PERSUASION OF PLACE

THE WORK OF
CECIL BAKER ARCHITECT

OSCAR RIERA OJEDA
PUBLISHERS

PERSUASION OF PLACE

THE WORK OF
CECIL BAKER ARCHITECT

Introduction & Text **Cheryl Weber**
Essays **Cecil Baker**
Edited **Oscar Riera Ojeda**
Principal Photography **Barry Halkin**

OSCAR RIERA OJEDA
PUBLISHERS

There is one person who has been my greatest source of inspiration, my most avid supporter, my humanizing coach – that is my friend and wife: Fairley Ross Baker. She saw my value when it was invisible to me. She coached and cajoled me, frustrated at my unwillingness to accept clients that I did not trust and assignments that I had lost patience with. She fundamentally saw much more in my work than I did.

TABLE OF CONTENTS

010 INTRODUCTION

SELECTED WORKS

016 THE NEST
028 SAG HARBOR RESIDENCE
042 YORK SQUARE
050 THE LIPPINCOTT
062 VAN PELT MEWS
070 URBAN TOWNHOUSES
076 JANNIE'S PLACE
082 FIRE ENGINE #37
090 SUZANNE & NORMAN COHN PHILADELPHIA CITY RESIDENCE
112 500 WALNUT
134 HORSESHOE BAY RESIDENCE
158 KOL EMET
166 MISSION GREEN
172 WESTERN UNION CONDOMINIUMS
180 HILARIE AND MITCHELL MORGAN RESIDENCE

200	ST. RITA PLACE & CASCIA CENTER
208	DUROVSIK RESIDENCE
230	ANDREW R. AND MINDY H. HEYER LOBBY
234	CHESTNUT HILL LIBRARY ADDITION
240	SUZANNE & NORMAN COHN, PRIMARY RESIDENCE
260	RIVERVIEW EXECUTIVE PARK
270	SOCIETY HILL RESIDENCE
280	JEFFERSON ACCELERATOR ZONE
284	ONE RIVERSIDE
298	BRIDGITTE MAYER GALLERY
302	NORTHERN HOME FOR CHILDREN
310	FRETZ SHOWROOM
314	POLICE FIRE HEADQUARTERS
322	JCHAI
332	FIRE ENGINE #38
340	RALSTON/MERCY-DOUGLASS HOUSE
346	ROLLING STOCK HALL
352	2110 WALNUT STREET
360	NEW COURTLAND ALLEGHENY CAMPUS
366	2100 HAMILTON

APPENDIX

384	FINDING MY PLACE
400	CLIENTS AND HEROES
414	COLLABORATORS & PROJECT CREDITS
424	BOOK CREDITS

INTRODUCTION

By Cheryl Weber

We are drawn to places that are distinctive, defined by their culture and how their buildings have been adapted to culture, climate, and topography. In a city like Philadelphia, historical events, too, are powerful forces that shape a sense of place. Bounded by the Schuylkill and Delaware Rivers on the west and east, this land, originally belonging to the Lenape Indian tribe, is thick with history and the ghosts of the American Revolution. William Penn knew it as a place of order, establishing a welcoming immigrant sanctuary whose urban grid and ubiquitous row houses have been copied in cities across the U.S. Cecil Baker knows it as a place where modernity and tradition struggle for dominion, as in most of America.

Baker is not a Quaker, but his approach to architecture has made him a good fit in the famous City of Brotherly Love. His buildings are progressive in the same way Penn and subsequent generations of Quakers have recognized their social and civic responsibilities. He has been described as honest, humble, and passionate, possessing a practical approach to getting things done. But, after studying under Louis Kahn at the University of Pennsylvania, practicality was not initially a trait to which he aspired. That would come from his firm's hardscrabble beginnings during the 1970s recession. By combining his considerable artistic talents with a knack for negotiation and a respect for his clients and his city, Baker has amassed a remarkable body of work that draws a line between Philadelphia's storied past and its future-facing present. From single-family homes and affordable housing to some of the city's most notable luxury towers, he has successfully found angles on old and new in a way that works for everyone.

To understand Baker's role in Philadelphia's architecture, you must understand its recent history. In the 1970s, the city entered a long downturn after a heady period of urban renewal in the 1950s and 1960s, orchestrated by urban planner Ed Bacon. New architecture during those decades was heavily influenced by Penn's architecture school and Dean G. Holmes Perkins' recruitment of young modernist faculty such as Ian McHarg, Louis Kahn, Robert Venturi, and Denise Scott Brown. For centuries, there had been a Classical consensus about beauty. The best civic buildings were associated with decorative columns and pedimented, symmetrical façades; now, noted architects were breaking all those rules. But just as Baker and his three partners were launching BRHB, the bubble burst. The recession arrived; the city began losing population and wouldn't recover for more than 20 years.

"Cecil is someone who stuck around through pretty seismic changes in the city's fortunes," says local journalist Jake Blumgart. "Then it picked up steam after the Great Recession and began to become a serious city."

With no work, what followed was a crash course in creating their own small development projects by building housing into derelict industrial buildings and rehabbing old townhouses in Queen Village, where some of the partners were living. Before long they began winning larger commissions for HUD Section 8 housing, including 131 townhouses and apartments scattered among infill and rehab sites in Washington Square West. When completed, these projects were indistinguishable from the neighborhood's market rate housing. "Some of the buildings we rehabbed were historically significant and had to meet the requirements of the historic commission," recalls BRHB partner Michael Horn. They also won a Section 8 competition for 50-some new housing units across a city block in Chinatown. Designed for recent immigrants from Hong Kong, the designs included interior courtyards for socializing. "The immigrant population who moved in loved it. They raised their children and even their grandchildren there," says Horn, who, with the partners, owned and managed the buildings for 30-some years.

"Cecil was building row houses at a time when very few people were doing it," says *Philadelphia Inquirer* architecture critic Inga Saffron. "When the city was in bad shape and almost nothing new was being built, he acted as developer. The city was still losing population

Unity is strength; when there is teamwork and collaboration, wonderful things can be achieved.

William Penn

right up until 2007; there was not a lot of real architecture being built, and very little residential. He kept the faith and believed in the city."

His work on "Turning on the Lights Upstairs" attests to that commitment. In the mid-1990s Paul Levy, then head of the Central Philadelphia Development Corp., hired him to study the feasibility of turning the vacant offices above street-level retail into housing – a condition many cities are facing today. Owners of these buildings often removed the stairs to gain more retail space, and with no access to the upper stories, the buildings were rotting from the top down. Cecil Baker and his team mined the possibilities of those empty upper stories. They evaluated 10 properties east of Broad Street and south of Chestnut and recommended tax code changes that would make their redevelopment economically possible.

"The project caught the attention of a range of people interested in development," Levy says. "It created a critical mass in which we worked with the Rendell administration to create a tax abatement for 10 years for conversion of any vacant office or industrial building to residential or hotel use." He adds: "Conversion of older buildings is often less expensive than building up, but most important it preserves great historic architecture. Cecil showed us how to do it. The tool spread and was used throughout the city; it added a dramatic amount of vitality to the downtown. We're ahead of so many other cities because of this."

City of Neighborhoods
Although Baker would go on to establish himself across well-funded institutional, commercial, and education commissions after opening a new architecture firm in 1982, he never forgot the early lessons in creating – with bare bones budgets – light-filled buildings that were forward-thinking while fitting into their historic context. How that basic belief worked out over the course of his career is clearly expressed in this book, particularly his work with developers. His adaptive reuse design for the highly visible Lippincott building, a 1900 landmark on Washington Square, ensured that it would live on as an icon on the edge of Society Hill. Knowing that other developers could not get the residential conversion to pencil out, Baker proposed adding three two-story penthouses to the existing five-story structure, since it had originally been engineered for seven floors. Each of the build-to-suit unit layouts is unique, and the penthouse level is set back so its massing is hidden from the street. Two decades later, "you rarely see a unit in that building come up for sale, and some of the original owners are still living there," says the developer, Jay Cramner.

"There is no broad brushstroke in Cecil's work," adds Cranmer, who has developed residential projects with him across the market spectrum. "Cecil tries to add something positive to the community at large. He knows the city and went around trying to do everything as well as it could be done. He was quietly principled, saying, 'This is how it ought to be.'"

His influence grew when he served as an advisor on the City Center Residents Association (CCRA) from 2012 to 2019. Covering much of downtown, it reviews proposed buildings over 100,000 square feet and represents some of the city's most recognizable locations. "Developers had to go to the zoning board, and if the CCRA was opposed, their likelihood of success was reduced," says Rick Gross, the association head who engaged Cecil to help developers improve their designs – an often-tricky proposition. "Cecil became something of a folk hero [in the community] because he criticized a lot of architects for their cookie cutter buildings," Saffron says. "Some architects did resent him for that, because they knew that he knew what constraints they were under. He used it as a soapbox to articulate some ideas about what good design was. Sometimes he could come off sounding overly righteous."

Sometimes his humor softened the message. "Baker became known for thoughtful, witty, and occasionally lacerating commentary at the committee meetings," Blumgart wrote in the *Philadelphia Inquirer*, adding,

"He critiqued the design of bay windows in many new developments as suffering from 'SpongeBob SquarePants syndrome.'"

One memorable project was the Harper, a 24-story upscale apartment tower at Rittenhouse Square whose developer had failed three times to get permission to exceed the statutory limits on height and density. "We said, the CCRA is prepared to make a deal with you if you work with the architect that we choose," Gross says. "We hired Cecil, who listened to our concerns and negotiated with the developer. Cecil redesigned it in a way that doesn't block views and changed the exterior and orientation. The front entrance incorporates some of the historic elements from the building that were there originally. Ultimately, the developer hired Cecil directly to finish the building. The neighborhood loves it, and it was an enormous success. We often avoided an extended legal fight by bringing a good architect to the table, and Cecil was the epitome of that."

It's a critical skill in older cities struggling to expand their tax base while preserving the essential urban fabric. "Philadelphia is poor and needs the money generated by big buildings and tenants that spend money," Gross says. "I think Center City has set a model for the right buildings in the right places and bringing scale, height, and modernism in a way that blends and doesn't offend. Cecil has a totally engaging personality and very strong views, but he doesn't articulate them in a way that puts people off. Center City has by and large retained the character that makes it so special, and I give Cecil credit for being part of that."

Increasingly, the projects brought before the CCRA were his own. Baker had first designed the ultra-luxury condo tower at 500 Walnut for a site on Rittenhouse Square. When the developer backed out, Baker approached Tom Scannapieco with the idea of adapting it for the Walnut Street site, directly behind Independence Hall. At 26 stories tall, the proposed building received pushback from Society Hill neighbors who had view, scale, and traffic concerns. Most significantly, it sat directly behind Independence Hall and within the view corridor of the Liberty Bell pavilion, from which park guides routinely pointed out the bell's previous perch atop Independence Hall.

"Cecil helped get approvals by creating a very sharp bevel in front on Walnut Street that preserved the blue sky around the bell tower of Independence Hall when standing directly behind the Liberty Bell," Scannapieco says. "At the groundbreaking ceremony he used his arm to chop through the air and said the cleaver of history impacted the design of this building. I thought introducing that triangle would ruin the interior space plan, but he worked the angle to make the interiors more interesting." (Indeed, it contains the most expensive home sold in the city's history.) Baker also satisfied community concerns by switching the entrance to the rear, connecting it to the residential fabric of Society Hill.

"This was a difficult project because there'd been lawsuits with tenants of the Penn Mutual building," Saffron says. "Their windows were going to be blocked and no one could figure out the design. He really sculpted a building that satisfied everybody. It was very slim, and I'm sure had a lot of difficult engineering because of that. He was a great mediator in that regard."

"If you went to central casting and wanted someone to play an architect, they would give you Cecil Baker; he carries that persona," Scannapieco says. "His personality is reflected in the architecture; he's not an in-your-face kind of person but very much a gentleman, sensitive to the people around him, thoughtful and respectful."

Discuss and Discern

Regardless of their type, scale, or setting, Baker's buildings artfully express the choreography and patterns of contemporary life. And they honor the local vernacular with subtlety, surprise, and presence. His design for Judith Creed Horizons for Achieving Independence (JCHAI), an administrative and educational facility for people with disabilities, is airy and welcoming. "Traditionally there have not been stand-alone buildings that work with such people who are just out of high school," says JCHAI founder Judith Creed. "What does exist is usually in the basement of other buildings, with no windows and kind of dreary. Our vision was to have something that was modern and high-tech and as good as it gets."

Its textured brickwork riffs on the predominantly brick buildings on the Jewish Federation of Greater Philadelphia campus in Bryn Mawr. Held between two steeply pitched volumes, the glassy entry portal opens to leafy views of the arboretum. "We were two women – a speech language pathologist and a film producer – with no experience in the area of building," says Creed. "It required a lot of trust, education, and patience from the architect, and Cecil provided it. He is an elegant, soft-spoken individual who makes eye contact and meets you where you are emotionally. I admire him as a human being and what he's contributed to the world of architecture, but most importantly, I really appreciate him for giving us this beautiful building that we continue to be proud of."

At Congregation Kol Emet, a synagogue in the suburb of Yardley, Baker created an expressive, light-filled building that imbues a centuries-old tradition with contemporary meaning. "Cecil didn't know much about synagogues but had done a lot of homework on synagogue buildings over the last 150 years," says Steve Gross, who was chair of the synagogue. "He was intellectually curious and became part of our fabric and journey in trying to understand what we wanted."

That process left an impression on Janice Woodcock, an architect in Baker's office at the time. "He would often get the committee to agree with itself rather than fighting with us," she says. "He got them to discuss and discern so they were comfortable with the direction before we designed anything." Woodcock also learned from Baker that some things are worth fighting for. When Inglis Gardens at Eastwick, which went on to win a national HUD award, came in over budget during the design phase, she began exploring a flat-roof design. "He got kind of mad, took the pen out of my hand, and put the roof back on," Woodcock recalls. "He wasn't going to have it and convinced the client to raise the budget. I never took a roof off again."

Former employee Alexandra Fazio also benefited from Baker's mentorship. "There's this thing, the gospel according to Cecil," she says. "He has a lot of opinions – about the choreography of passage, how users move through space, and how architecture changes their experience. It's about how a building is laid out and its proportions, but also details like where a light switch is placed on a wall, whether a door would swing in or out of a space, and how close to the wall it would be. That the things a user touches are just as important as the things they see with their eyes."

It's these qualities that caught the eye of patrons Suzanne and Norman Cohn, who over the years have commissioned bespoke homes in Philadelphia, Florida, and New York. Their first project with Baker was an 8,700-square-foot penthouse and outdoor terrace overlooking Washington Square Park. He integrated their significant art collection while assiduously avoiding the feeling of a museum. The design creates a sense of discovery and intimacy, an interior experience that shifts with the time of day, movement from room to room, and quality of lighting. "He has a natural love for materials and lighting and manipulates them to enhance space," says Suzanne Cohn. "I think he is a profound listener, but he also has the fortitude to say, 'Suzanne, I don't think that's going to work. Let's try something else.' Then I knew that when he affirmed what I wanted, it was going to be good."

In *The Architecture of Happiness*, Alain de Botton wrote, "One of the great but often unmentioned causes of both happiness and misery is the quality of our environment: the kinds of light, rooms, buildings, and streets that surround us." This monograph is a tour through buildings that embody that philosophy. Featured projects represent the broad range of work that Baker and his firm embraced. It's worth noting that few architects routinely take on the spectrum of residential buildings that Baker did throughout his career. As with the luxury towers, he brought rigorous design to market-rate and subsidized housing, where the accountants were often in charge. "A lot of multifamily apartment buildings are designed by a developer who will flip it," Saffron says. "It's not designed to be passed down to their kids the way merchant builders of old did. Investors want their 6 percent return, and you just turn the screws until you make the numbers work. They don't care; it's not their city. I know Cecil struggled to make them decent. Cecil did work hard to do the details. He is a real architect who came from the old days."

Indeed, it is particulars that interest Baker and define his firm's architecture. Every project filtered his resonant memories and his clients' goals through the prism of good design. For all the differences between, say, Sag Harbor Residence, the Cohn penthouse, and Inglis Gardens, it is clear that all his buildings emerge from the same place. What they share, in the end, is a balance between symmetry and asymmetry, abstract and specific, and an appreciation for light, context, and simple forms. It is the eloquence of these qualities that explains Cecil Baker best of all.

Cheryl Weber has written extensively on houses and architecture firms for national magazines and as a former book editor has commissioned and produced numerous books on architecture and landscape architecture. She is coauthor of *Concrete Houses: Form, Line, and Plane*.

SELECTED WORKS

THE NEST

STUDENT HOUSING SERVING TEMPLE UNIVERSITY, PHILADELPHIA, PA

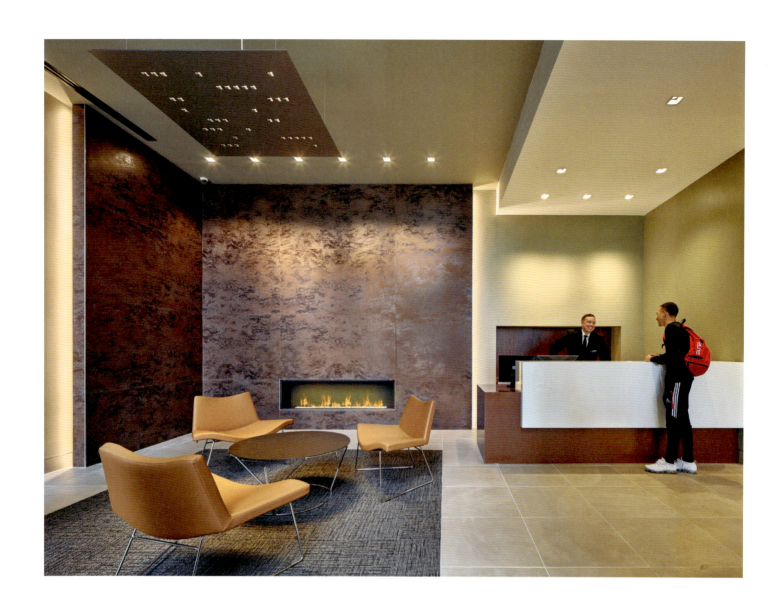

SELECTED WORKS　　　　　　　　　　　THE NEST　　　　　　　　　　　025

SAG HARBOR RESIDENCE

NEW BEACHFRONT CUSTOM RESIDENCE,
NOYACK, NY

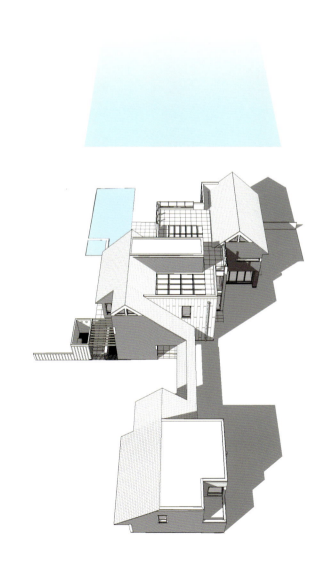

SELECTED WORKS — SAG HARBOR RESIDENCE — 033

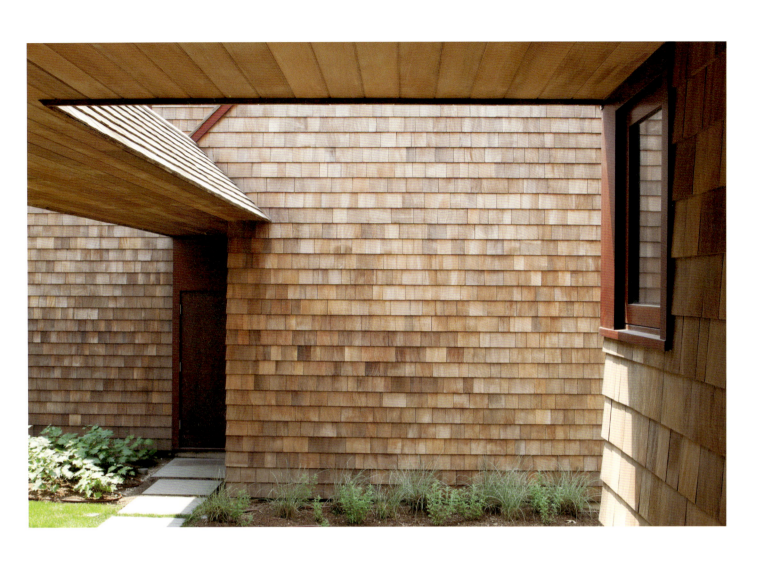

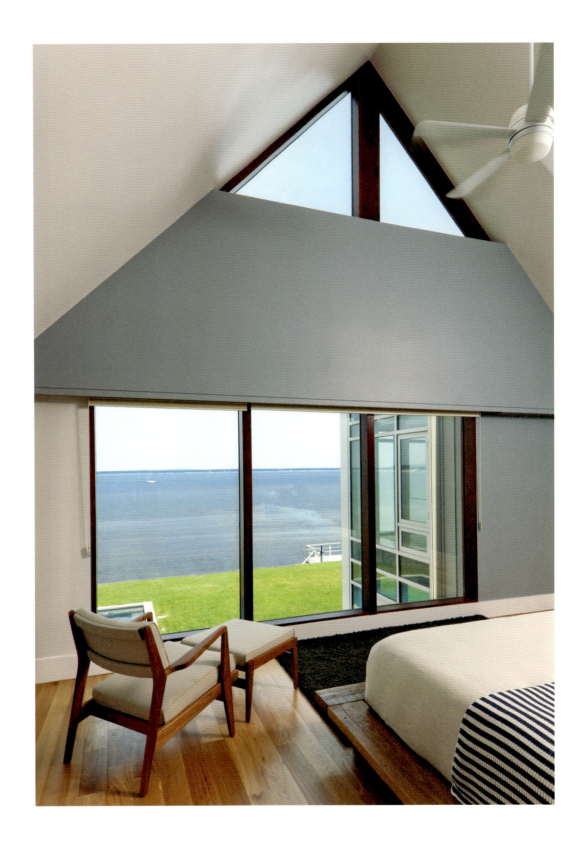

YORK SQUARE

NEW 60 UNIT CONDOMINIUM STRUCTURE
IN HISTORIC INDUSTRIAL NEIGHBORHOOD,
PHILADELPHIA, PA

"York Square Condominiums is an excellent example of urban infill, developed with community involvement and public support. It is recognized for an exemplary site plan that re-establishes the fabric of the neighborhood with safe and attractive pedestrian frontage on three sides." 1,000 Friends of Pennsylvania, 2004 Design Award winner.

SELECTED WORKS — YORK SQUARE — 047

THE LIPPINCOTT

ADAPTIVE REUSE AND OVERBUILD OF
HISTORIC PUBLISHING HOUSE,
BUILD-TO-SUIT CONDOMINIUMS,
PHILADELPHIA, PA

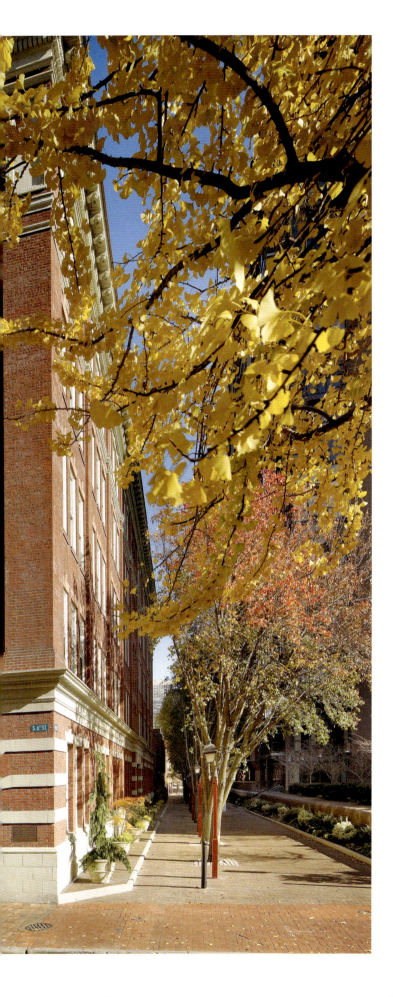

"Each room in a Cecil Baker + Partners design feels complete and yet, in what they call the choreography of passage, some asymmetrical moment will draw the viewer to experience the next room – a purposeful restlessness. They create quiet theater: spaces that slip from sanctuary to mystery, that remain in the mind like chapters in a book."

"Compression and expansion, the introduction of diffused natural light, materials that blur distinctions between floor, wall, or ceiling planes, and subtle shifts in color – these are the hallmarks of a Cecil Baker + Partners home." *Spectacular Homes of Greater Philadelphia*

SELECTED WORKS — THE LIPPINCOTT — 057

VAN PELT MEWS

ADAPTIVE REUSE OF HISTORIC CARRIAGE HOUSE AND 8 NEW RESIDENCES, PHILADELPHIA, PA

SELECTED WORKS

063

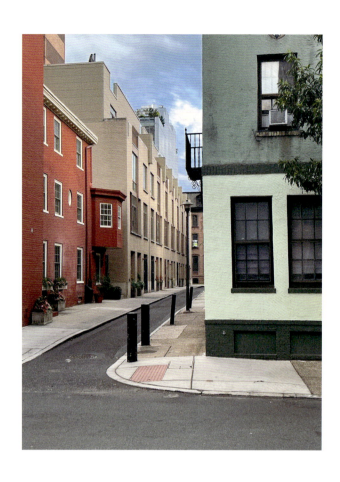

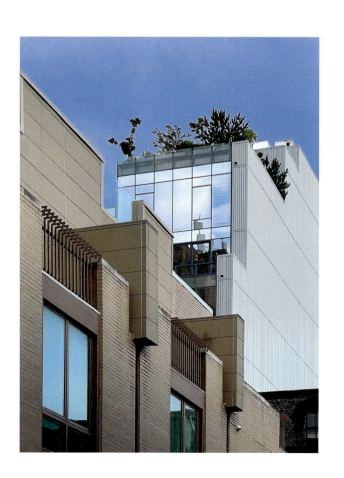

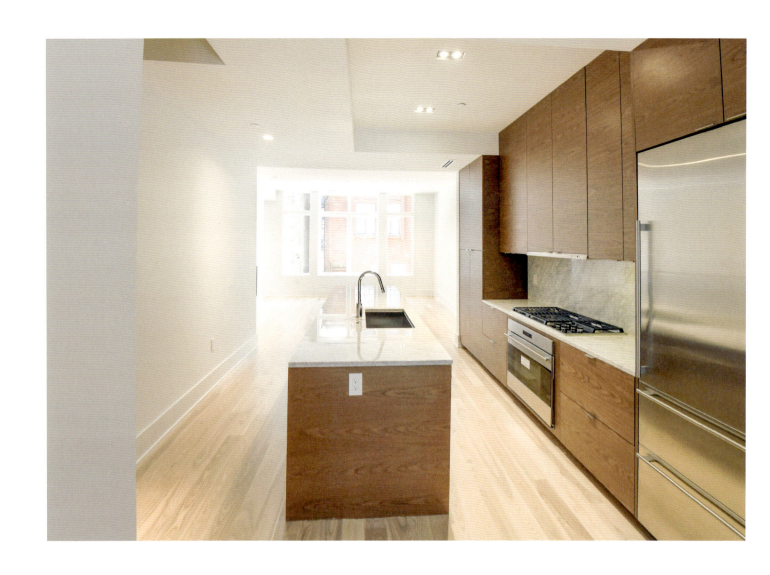

SELECTED WORKS   VAN PELT MEWS

URBAN TOWNHOUSES

THREE RESIDENCES,
WASHINGTON SQUARE WEST,
PHILADELPHIA, PA

"There is a cool hipness to the materials of these townhouses, an enterprising use of multi-textured industrial products, such as brick cement block, diamond plate, corrugated fiberglass and wrought iron. There is also a reimagining of form within the very limited construct of a "row house" – a playing with architectural language or vocabulary, including references to specific elements of the surrounding 19th century buildings, making for a contextual jumping-off point … This is savvy design that has a sense of humor as well as style, referring to its context, yet still making its own statement." Hip and Hidden Philadelphia, Virginia Restmeyer & E. I. Weiner

"This is a project that is a modern interpretation of the adjacent architecture along the street. The detailing is pretty exquisite. The texture and materials on the exterior and the time and thought that went into the interior detailing is pretty phenomenal." Betsy Beaman, AIA Philadelphia Awards Jury

"This Architect has contributed to a great tradition of infill construction in Philadelphia … probably done better than in any other city in the country…" AIAPa 2000 Awards Jury

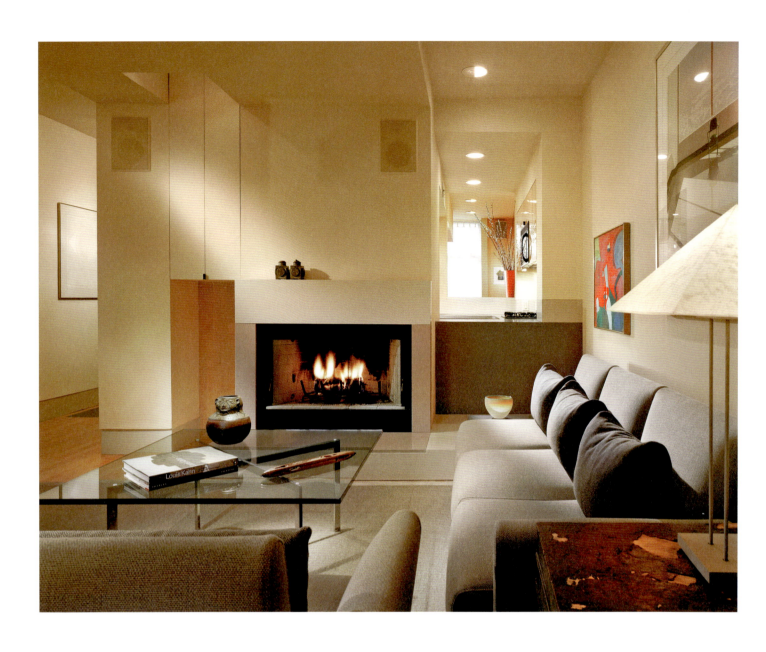

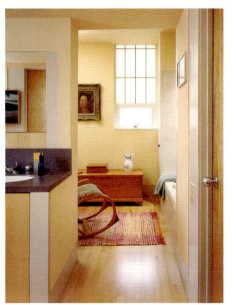

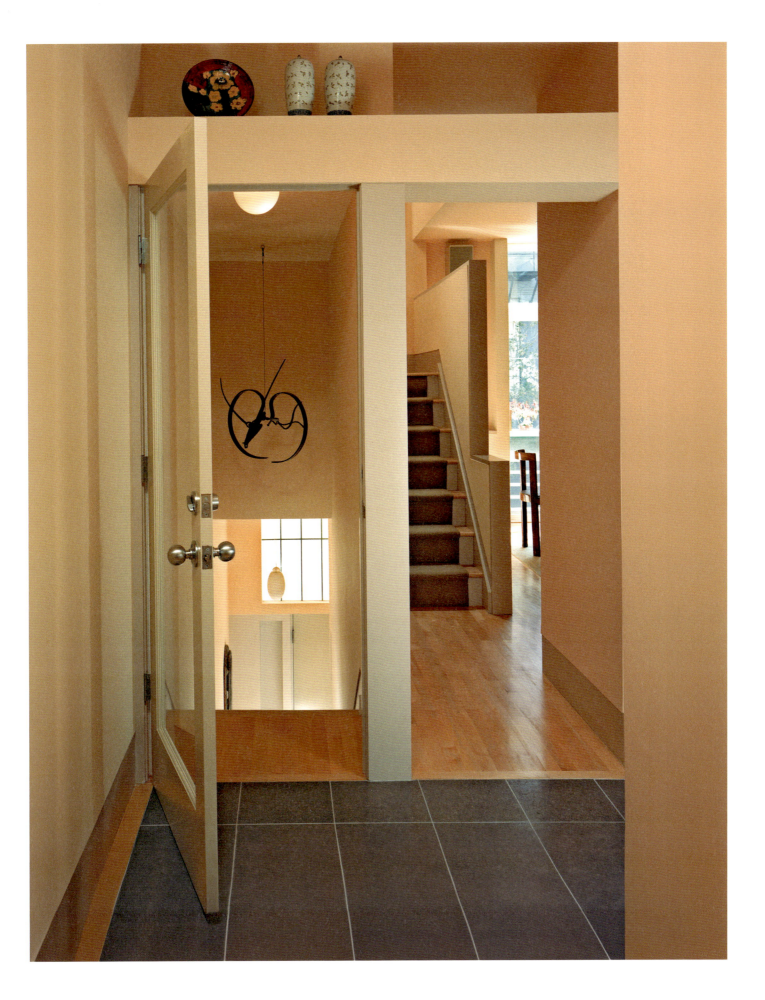

JANNIE'S PLACE

AFFORDABLE HOUSING & SUPPORTIVE SERVICES FOR SINGLE MOTHERS W/CHILDREN, PHILADELPHIA, PA

SELECTED WORKS JANNIE'S PLACE 079

FIRE ENGINE #37

RENOVATION AND ADDITION TO
HISTORIC FIREHOUSE,
CHESTNUT HILL,
PHILADELPHIA, PA

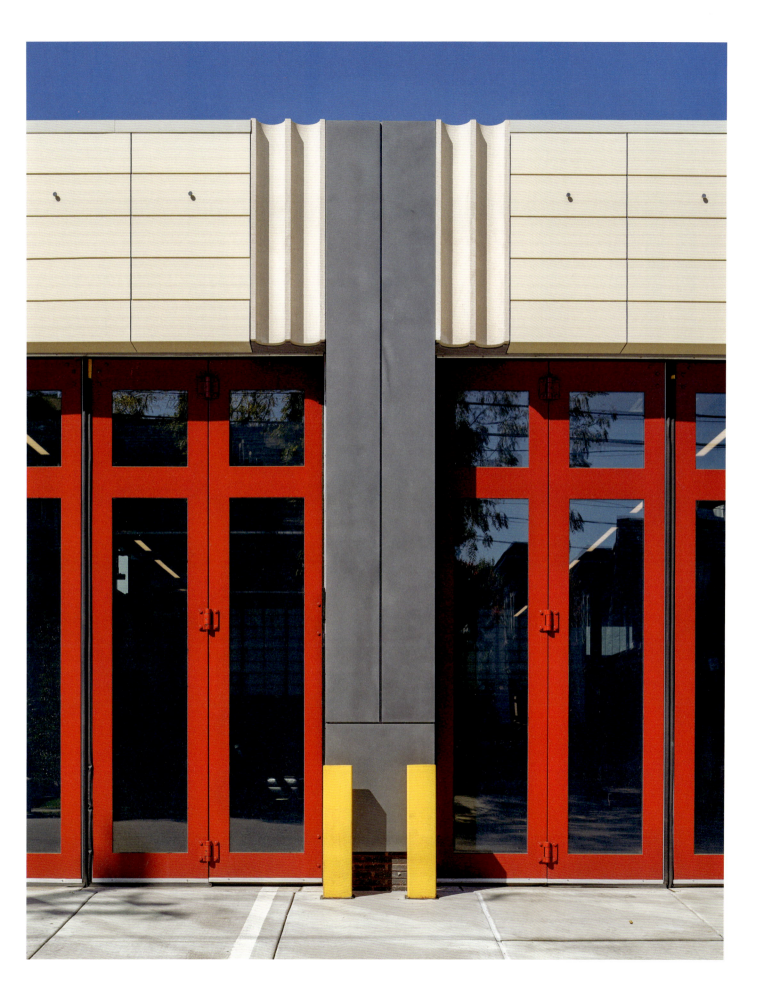

SELECTED WORKS FIRE ENGINE # 37 087

SUZANNE & NORMAN COHN
PHILADELPHIA CITY RESIDENCE

CUSTOM PENTHOUSE,
SOCIETY HILL,
PHILADELPHIA, PA

"There is nothing to compare with the incredible job you did for Norman and Suzanne Cohn! I can't get the place out of my head. I think it has to be among the most spectacular homes in the U.S. Suzanne said something to the effect that most people don't end up as fond of, and as close to their architect as they have to you." Suzanne and Ralph Roberts

"A hallmark of his residential work … is its mix of calming symmetry and restless asymmetry." Cheryl Weber, *Residential Architect*

SELECTED WORKS　　　　　SUZANNE & NORMAN COHN PHILADELPHIA CITY RESIDENCE　　　095

SELECTED WORKS · SUZANNE & NORMAN COHN PHILADELPHIA CITY RESIDENCE · 099

SELECTED WORKS SUZANNE & NORMAN COHN PHILADELPHIA CITY RESIDENCE 103

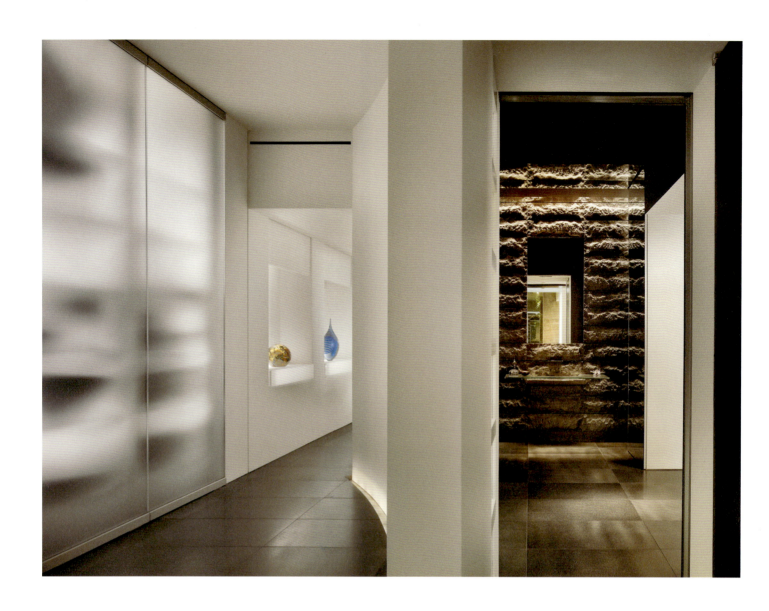

SELECTED WORKS　　　SUZANNE & NORMAN COHN PHILADELPHIA CITY RESIDENCE　　　109

500 WALNUT

RESIDENTIAL CONDOMINIUM TOWER
ON INDEPENDENCE NATIONAL HISTORIC PARK,
PHILADELPHIA, PA

"An extraordinary contribution to the City. A very handsome building and an ornament to Society Hill, even though it stands in contrast to historic materials from the 18th and 19th century. It does its job beautifully."
David Schaaf, Director of Urban Design, Philadelphia Planning Commission

SELECTED WORKS 500 WALNUT

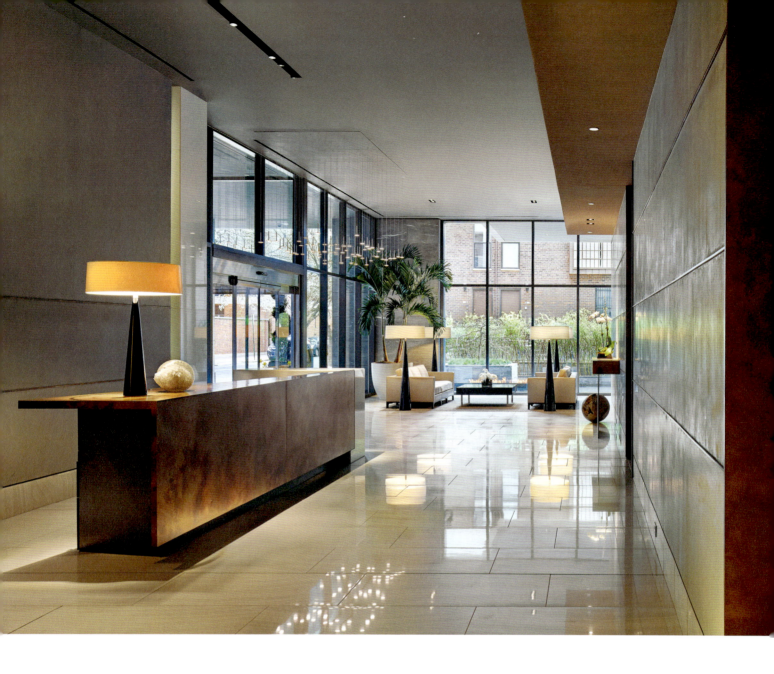

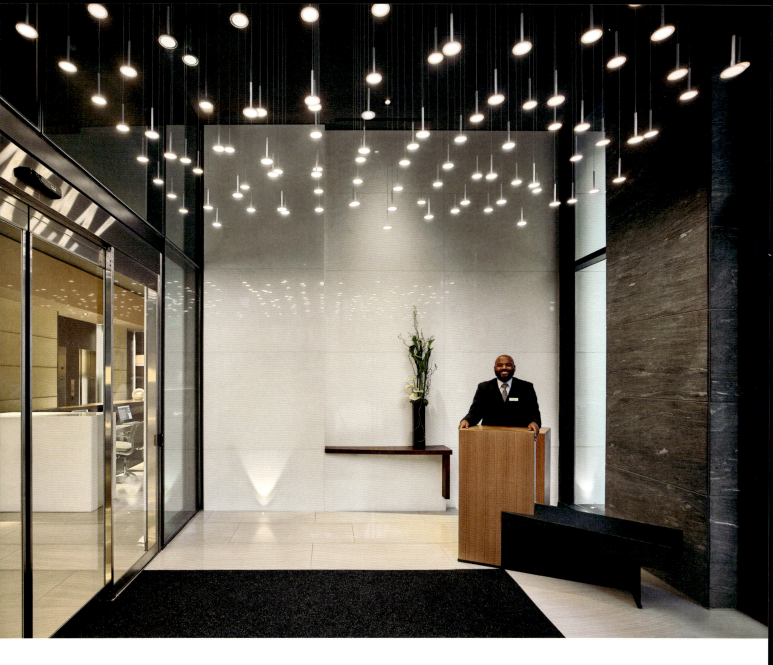

HORSESHOE BAY RESIDENCE
NEW CUSTOM RESIDENCE, TX

"I see complexities in shapes, spaces, colors, textures, masses, voids and experiences. To be sure, there is deliberateness and sophistication in these spaces and complexities. My eyes never tire of seeing what's around the corner."

Sam Drago

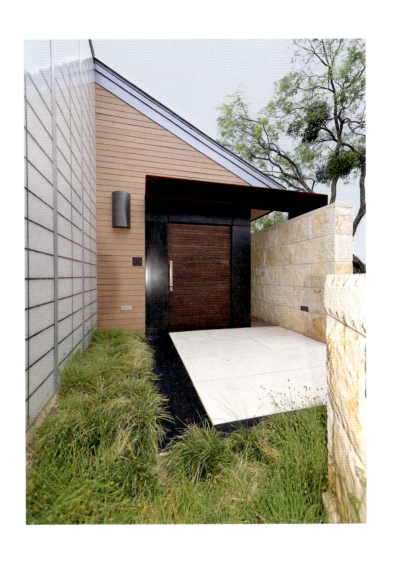

SELECTED WORKS   HORSESHOE BAY RESIDENCE   139

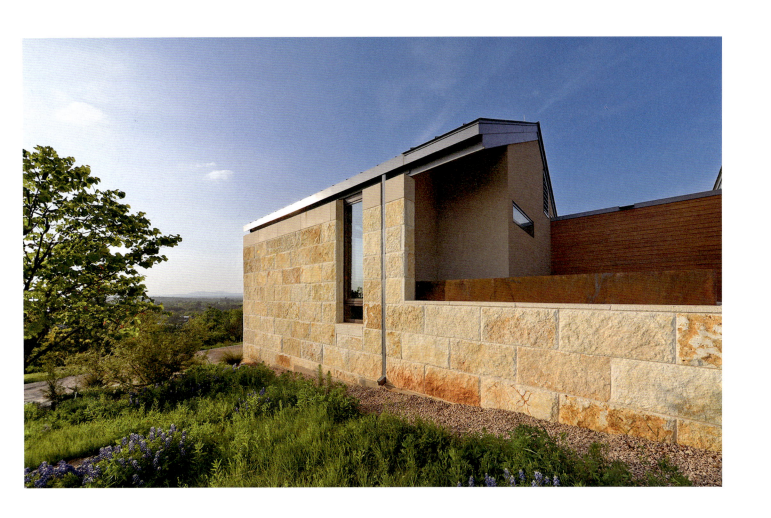

SELECTED WORKS   HORSESHOE BAY RESIDENCE

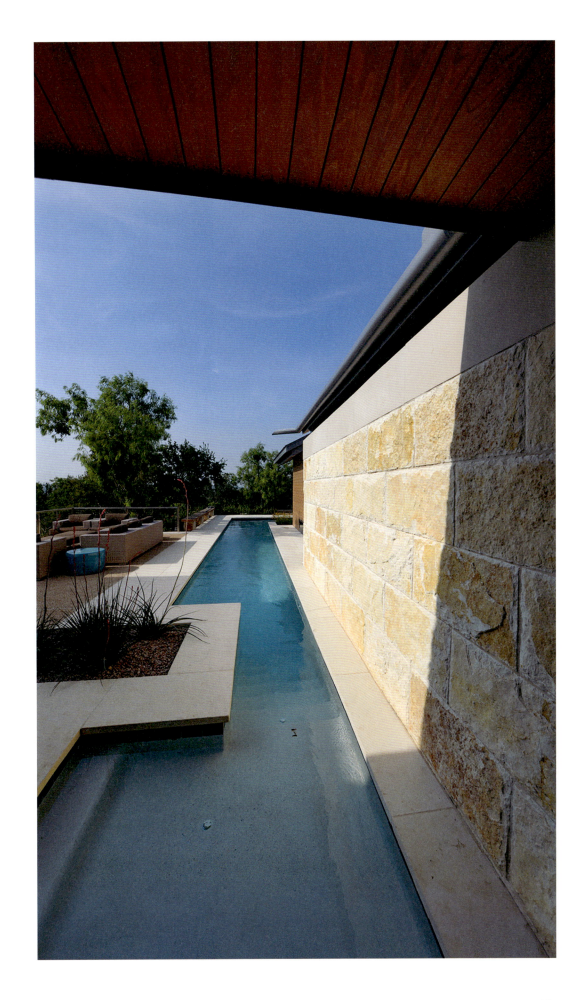

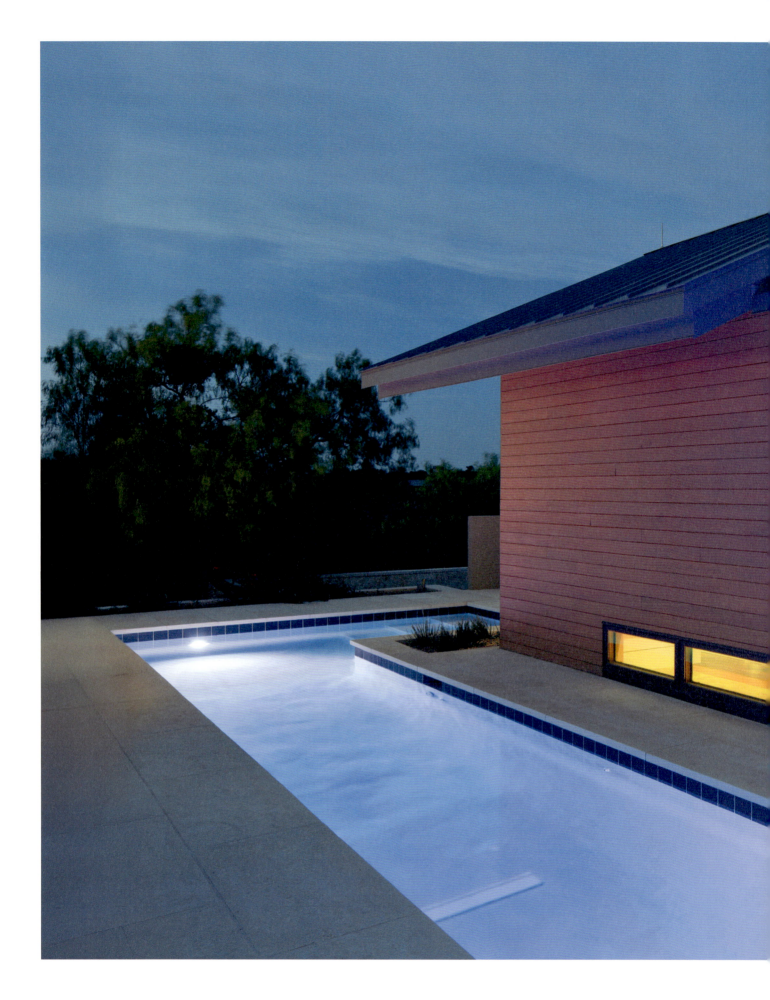

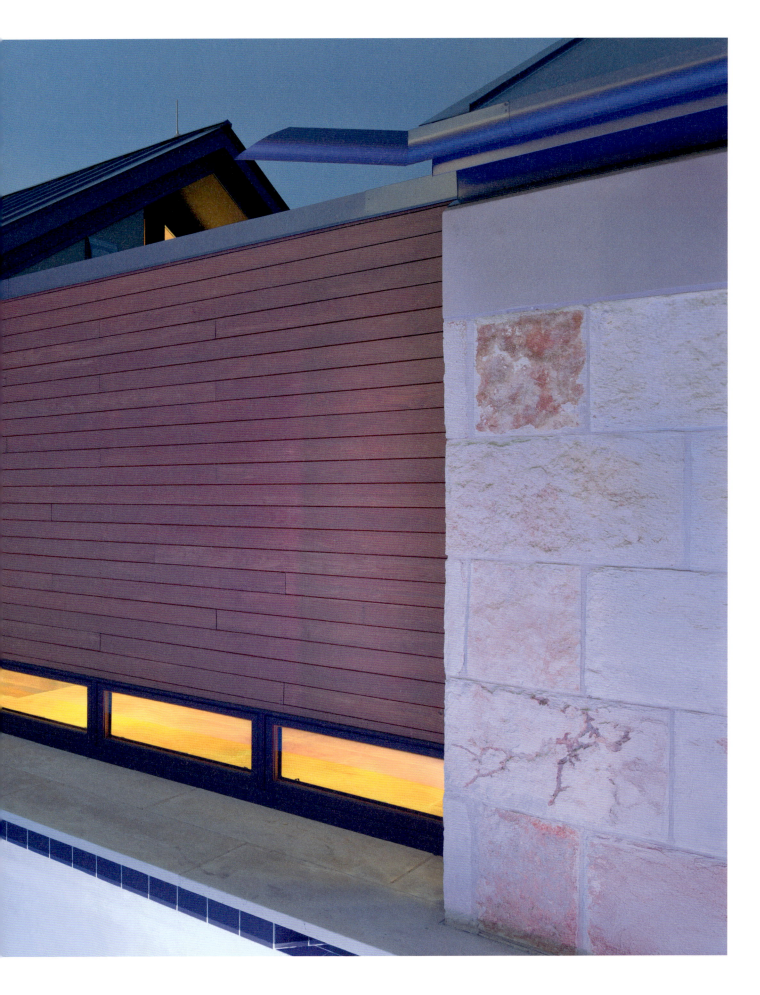

KOL EMET

NEW SYNAGOGUE AND SCHOOL, YARDLEY, PA

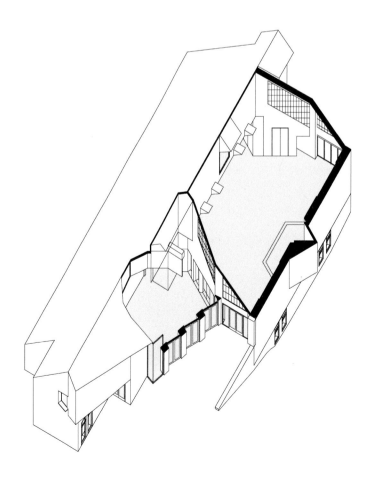

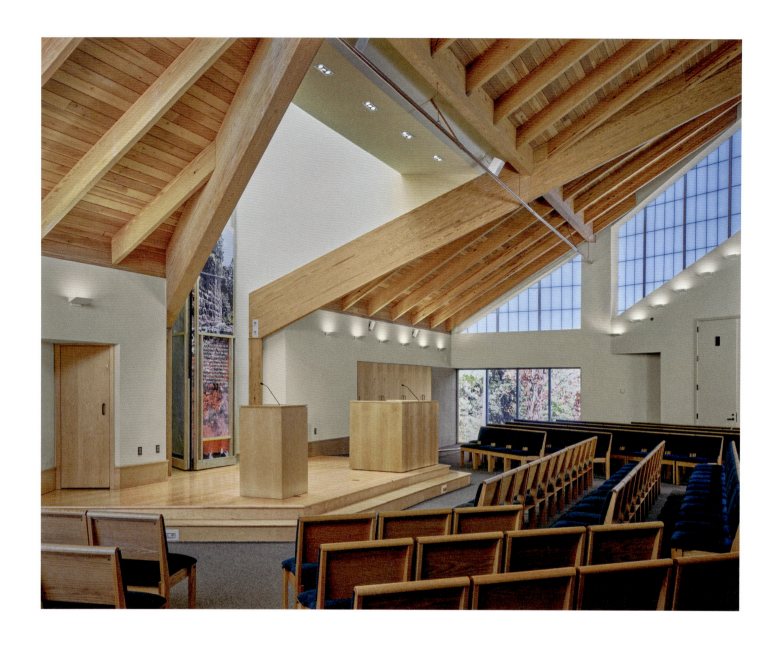

"It is a small miracle that a modest recently constructed synagogue in Lower Makefield Township has managed to triumph over its seclusion … the building makes sense on its own terms." Changing Skyline, Inga Saffron, The Philadelphia Inquirer

MISSION GREEN

61 AFFORDABLE UNITS ON 69 ACRE CAMPUS,
FOX CHASE, PA

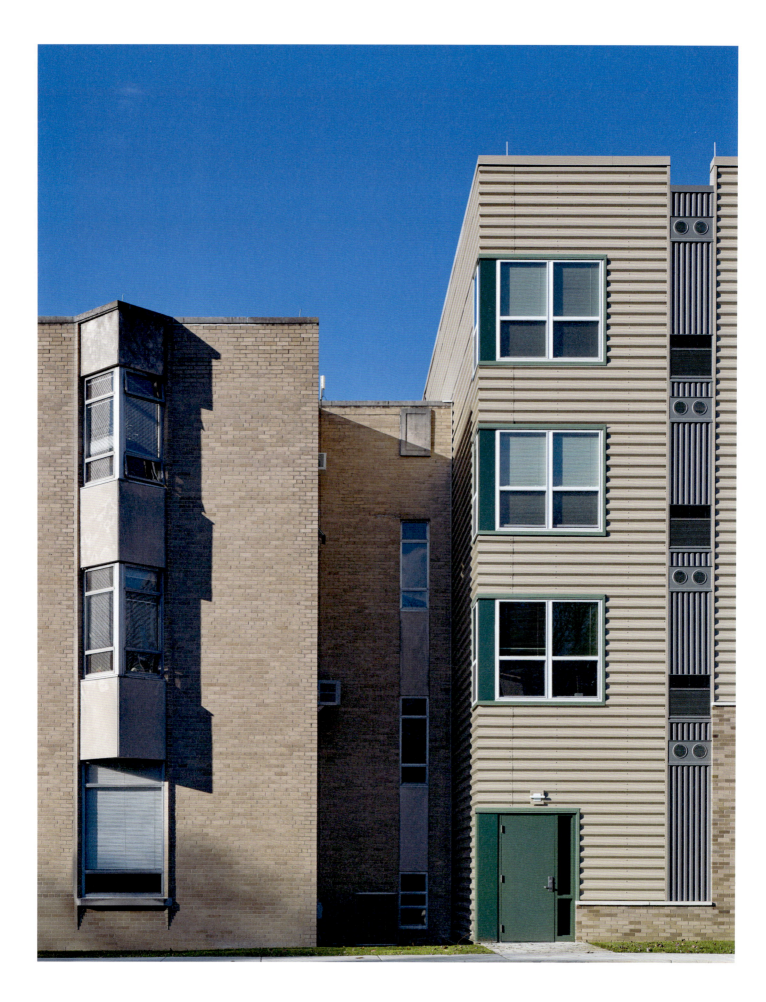

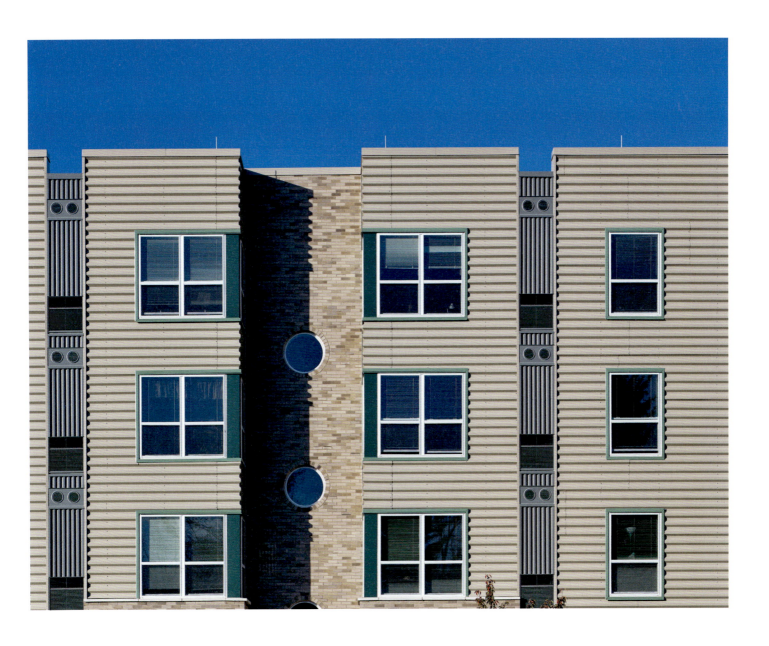

"Your gentle, quiet guidance of our Mission Green project is very much appreciated. I love the way the two buildings complement each other as though they belong together. I admire your sensitivity to form, line, design and color."

Sister Frankie Vaughn

WESTERN UNION CONDOMINIUMS

ADAPTIVE REUSE AND OVERBUILD
OF HISTORIC STRUCTURE INTO
100 LUXURY CONDOMINIUMS,
PHILADELPHIA, PA

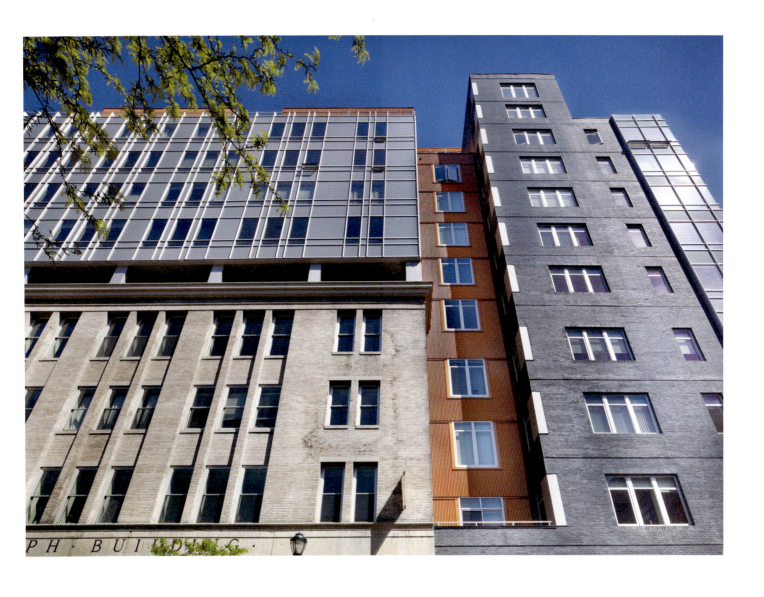

"I think your plans for the Western Union Building are absolutely marvelous. ...it's an assertion of urban scale in a way that the Victory building isn't, and I congratulate you on really introducing a new face for architecture."

Ed Bacon

HILARIE AND MITCHELL MORGAN RESIDENCE

RECONFIGURATION AND RENOVATION
OF A TWO STORY CONDOMINIUM
ON RITTENHOUSE SQUARE,
PHILADELPHIA, PA

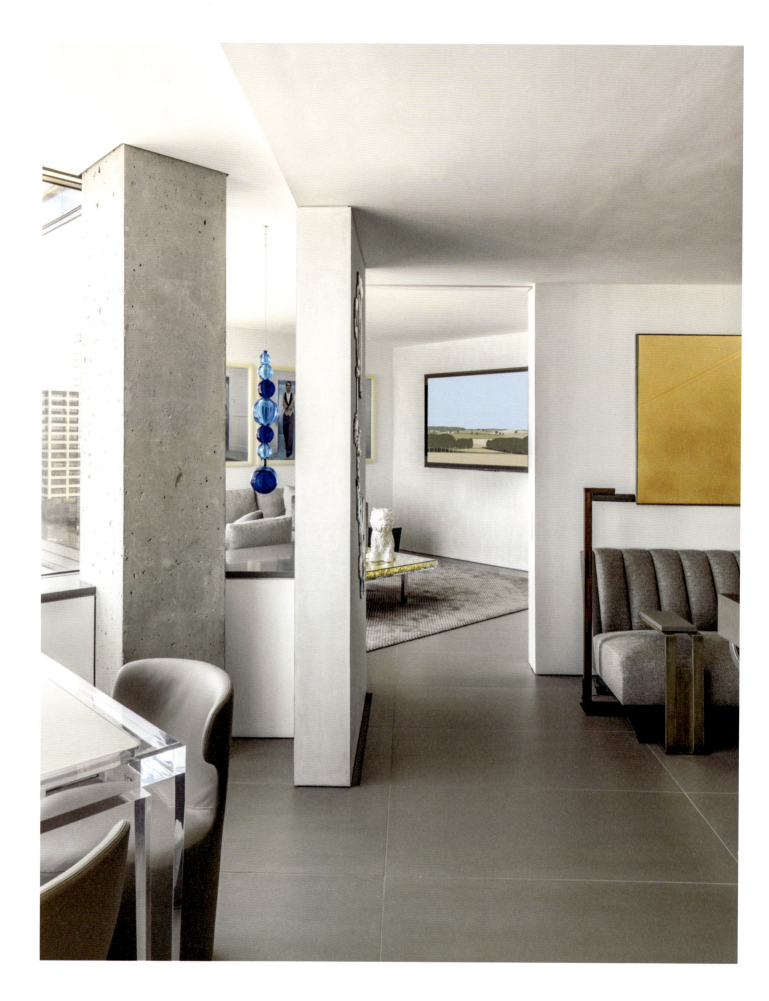

ST. RITA PLACE & CASCIA CENTER

AFFORDABLE SENIOR HOUSING AND CENTER FOR VISITING PILGRIMS, PHILADELPHIA, PA

"You have always established a bar much higher than the typical affordable design, so we always want to have you on our projects. And, even within our constrained budgets, you always manage to do better. Congratulations on making my built environment so much better to live and work in."
Roy Diamond, Diamond & Associates, affordable housing development advisory services

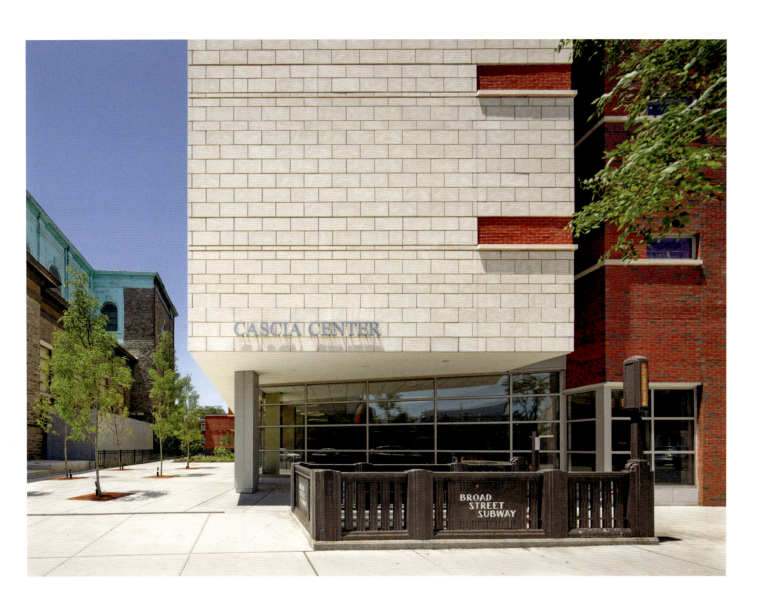

SELECTED WORKS ST. RITA PLACE & CASCIA CENTER 203

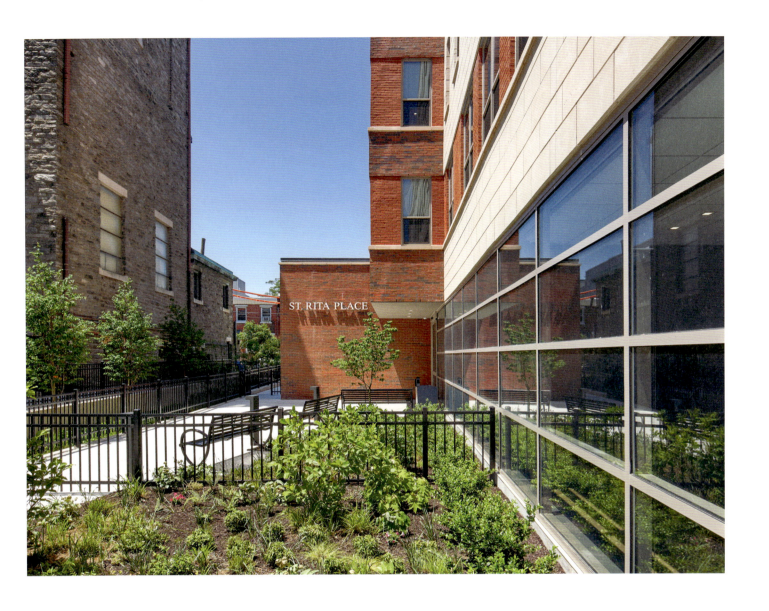

SELECTED WORKS ST. RITA PLACE & CASCIA CENTER

DUROVSIK RESIDENCE

NEW RESIDENCE WITHIN AND OVER A
HISTORIC CENTER CITY CARRIAGE HOUSE,
PHILADELPHIA, PA

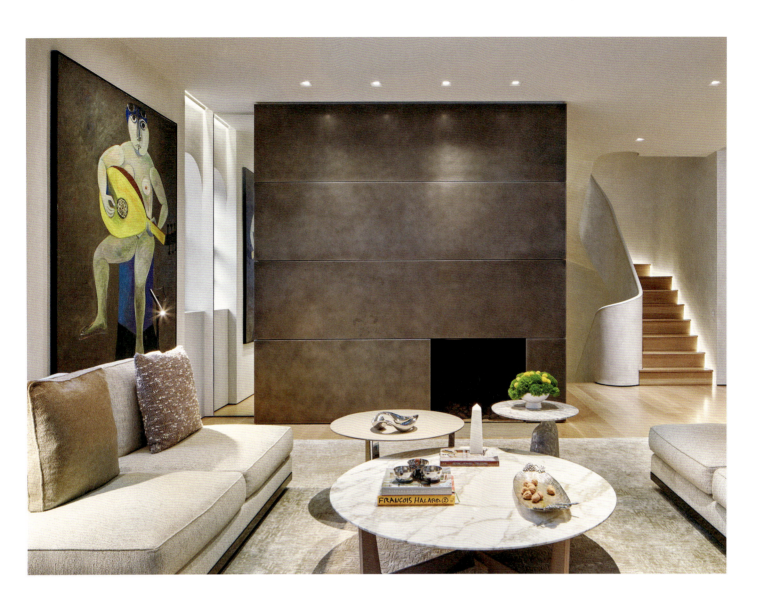

SELECTED WORKS — DUROVSIK RESIDENCE

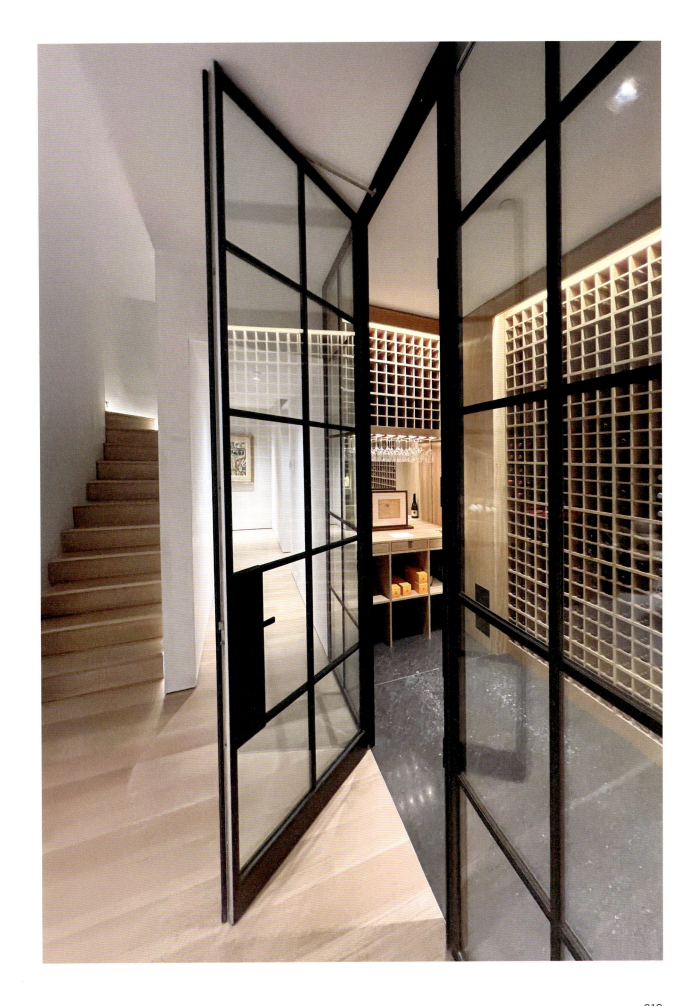

SELECTED WORKS DUROVSIK RESIDENCE

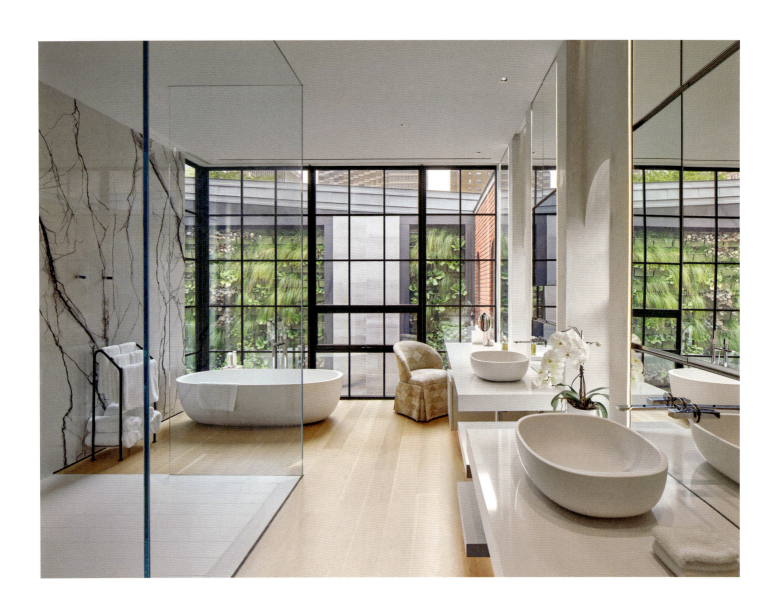

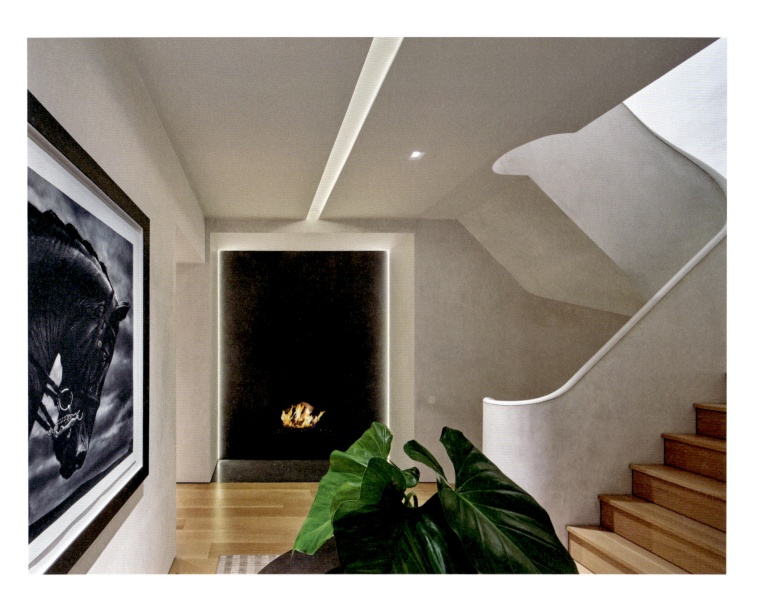

SELECTED WORKS — DUROVSIK RESIDENCE

ANDREW R. AND MINDY H. HEYER LOBBY

NEW LOBBY AND WAITING AREAS
FOR MATHEW J. RYAN VETERINARY HOSPITAL,
PHILADELPHIA, PA

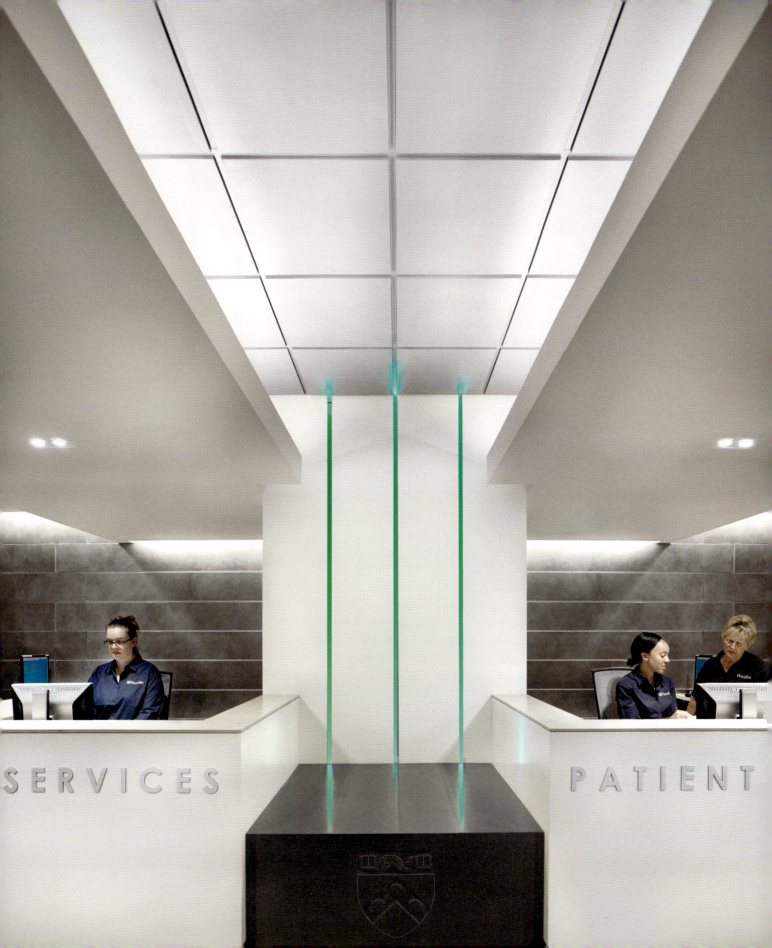

CHESTNUT HILL LIBRARY ADDITION

ADDITION TO A HISTORIC CARNEGIE LIBRARY, PHILADELPHIA, PA

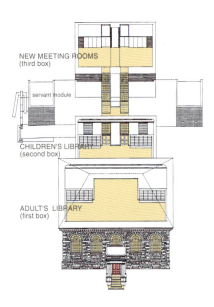

NEW MEETING ROOMS
(third box)

servant module

CHILDREN'S LIBRARY
(second box)

ADULT'S LIBRARY
(first box)

"A third box in a series brings the narrative of two earlier structures to a quiet resolution. The interiors are very pleasant and controlled. The proportions of every element are carefully thought out. Subdued and elegant." AIA Awards Jury

SELECTED WORKS CHESTNUT HILL LIBRARY ADDITION 237

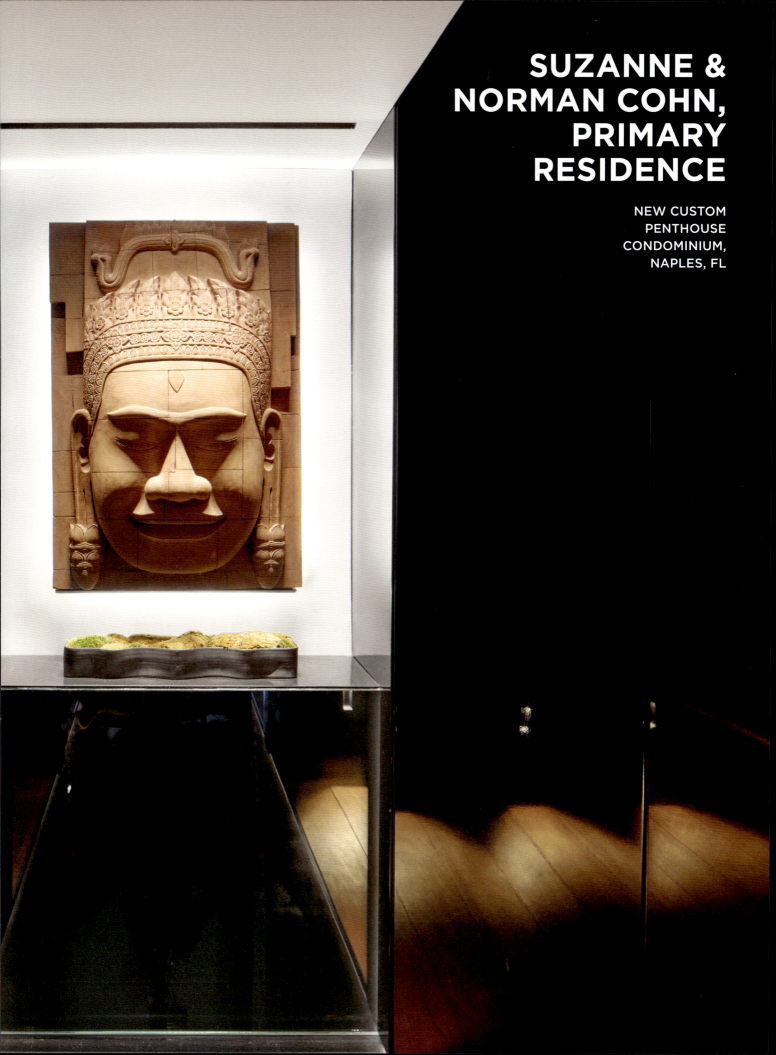

SUZANNE & NORMAN COHN, PRIMARY RESIDENCE

NEW CUSTOM PENTHOUSE CONDOMINIUM, NAPLES, FL

SELECTED WORKS SUZANNE & NORMAN COHN, PRIMARY RESIDENCE 243

SELECTED WORKS SUZANNE & NORMAN COHN, PRIMARY RESIDENCE 245

"This is sensational. Your creativity and design continue to amaze me."
Bud Hirsch

"That is magnificent!"
Bart Blatstein

SELECTED WORKS　　　　　　　　　　　　　　　　SUZANNE & NORMAN COHN, PRIMARY RESIDENCE　　　253

RIVERVIEW EXECUTIVE PARK

300,000 SF OFFICE COMPLEX FOR
THE NJ DEPARTMENT OF TREASURY,
TRENTON, NJ

SOCIETY HILL RESIDENCE

RENOVATION OF THE ZEEBOOKER RESIDENCE,
A MITCHELL GIURGOLA TOWNHOUSE,
PHILADELPHIA, PA

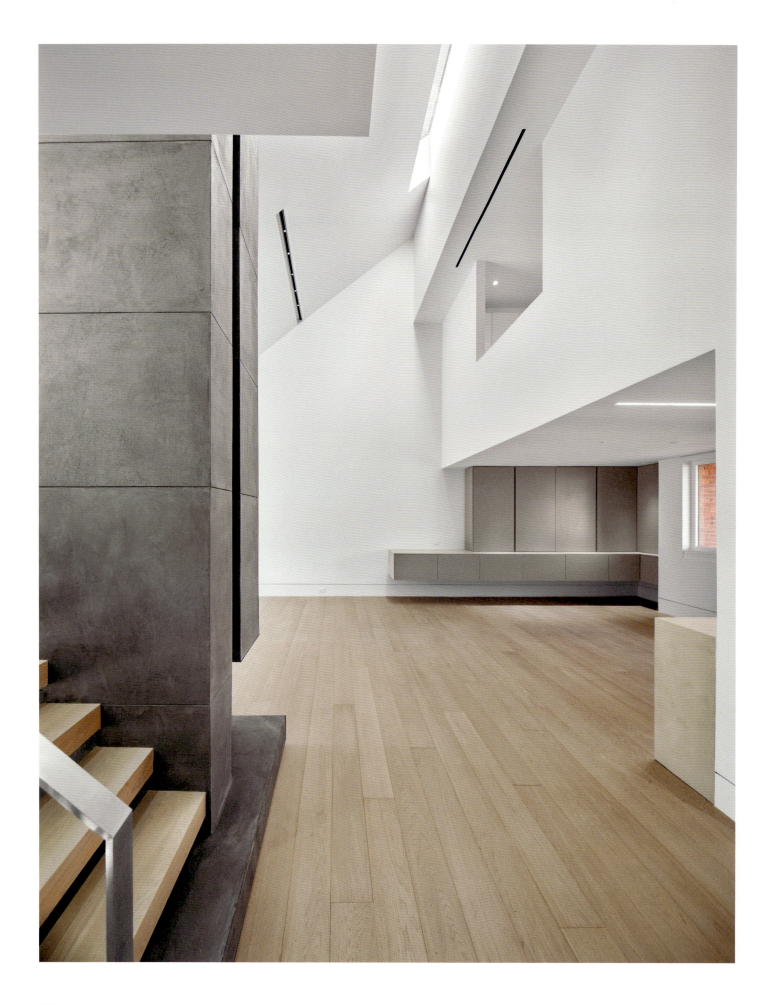

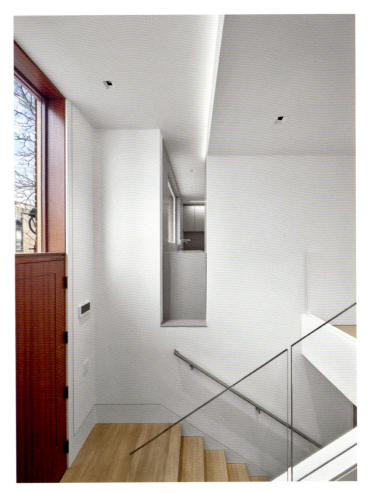

SOCIETY HILL RESIDENCE

JEFFERSON ACCELERATOR ZONE

INNOVATION AND RESEARCH CENTER
FOR THOMAS JEFFERSON UNIVERSITY,
PHILADELPHIA, PA

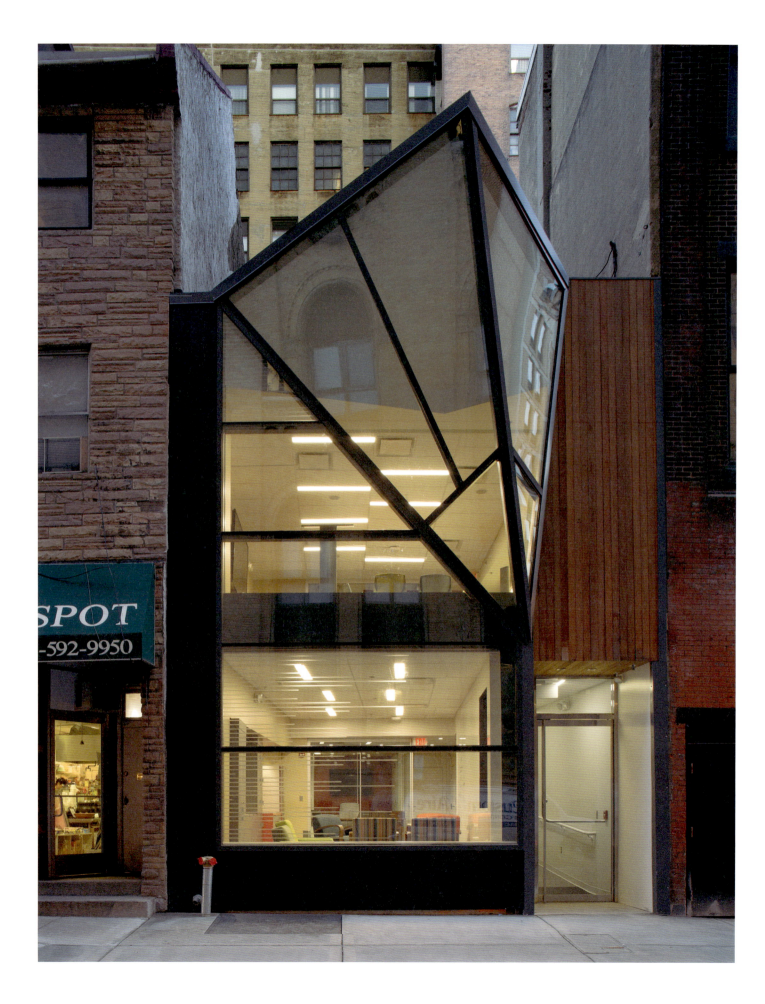

"The nature of the (City) grid makes it challenging for a building to stand out. But not impossible. Take a stroll along 10th Street, between Sansom and Walnut, and you'll encounter a small, but profound, aberration, a wrinkle in the smooth urban canvas. What was once the most bland of two-story brick buildings has been transformed into a delightful piece of sculpture. The unusual facade designed by Cecil Baker + Partners is not the sort of otherworldly spaceship that a Frank Gehry or a Zaha Hadid might land on a wide open site somewhere in Los Angeles or Paris. Baker's sculpture is squeezed onto a narrow lot between two typical 19th century Philadelphia workhorse buildings. It literally has to thrust itself into the public's field of view to get noticed."

"... as the glass climbs up the front wall, it begins to fan out, forming an off kilter crystal that bursts through the building plane, turning the row-house facade into a three dimensional object. The protrusion extends just three feet over the sidewalk - the legal limit - but you can't miss it." Changing Skyline, Inga Saffron, *Philadelphia Inquirer*

ONE RIVERSIDE

SIXTY-EIGHT UNIT LUXURY CONDOMINIUM
TOWER ON THE SCHUYLKILL RIVER,
PHILADELPHIA, PA

SELECTED WORKS · ONE RIVERSIDE · 289

"Dranoff credits his architects at Cecil Baker + Partners for their creativity in re-imagining the project. John Randolph, an architect, agreed: 'It was an amazing process. I felt Carl Dranoff listened carefully,'" Changing Skyline, Inga Saffron, *Philadelphia Inquirer*

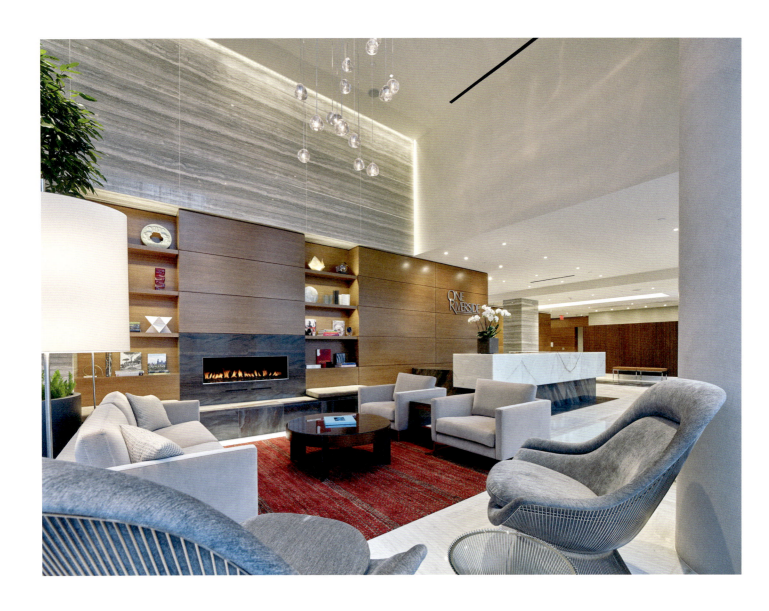

BRIDGITTE MAYER GALLERY

URBAN ART GALLERY LOCATED
IN HISTORIC SANSOM ROW,
SOCIETY HILL,
PHILADELPHIA, PA

SELECTED WORKS · BRIDGITTE MAYER GALLERY

BUCK AND WEINBERG RESIDENCE HALLS, NORTHERN HOME FOR CHILDREN

ADAPTIVE REUSE OF HISTORIC STRUCTURE WITH NEW ADDITION TO SERVE YOUNG MOTHERS IN NEED, PHILADELPHIA, PA

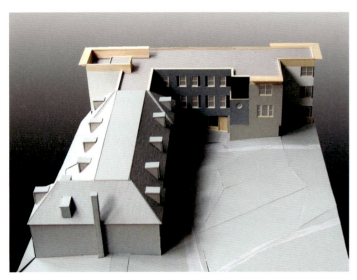

SELECTED WORKS — BUCK AND WEINBERG RESIDENCE HALLS, NORTHERN HOME FOR CHILDREN

SELECTED WORKS — BUCK AND WEINBERG RESIDENCE HALLS, NORTHERN HOME FOR CHILDREN

FRETZ SHOWROOM

42,000 SF SHOWROOM AND
CORPORATE HEADQUARTERS,
NAVAL YARD,
PHILADELPHIA, PA

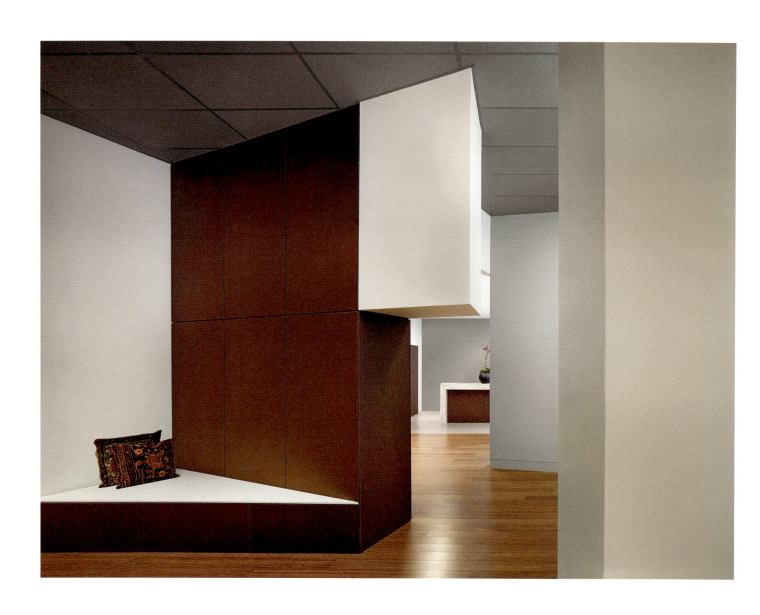

SELECTED WORKS • FRETZ SHOWROOM

POLICE FIRE HEADQUARTERS

50,000 SF MUNICIPAL FACILITY FOR
THE CITY OF PHILADELPHIA,
PHILADELPHIA, PA

"... the Siamese twin nature of the users appears to have been challenged, rebuffed and still resolved in a way that offers continuity and respect to the residential neighborhood."

"Interplay of volume, tone and color – explicit yet unique." AIA Awards Jury

"Very simple in volume ... very refined detailing that breaks down its scale..."
AIAPa 2000 Awards

JCHAI

ADMINISTRATIVE AND EDUCATIONAL FACILITY
FOR ADULTS WITH DEVELOPMENTAL DISABILITIES,
RADNOR, PA

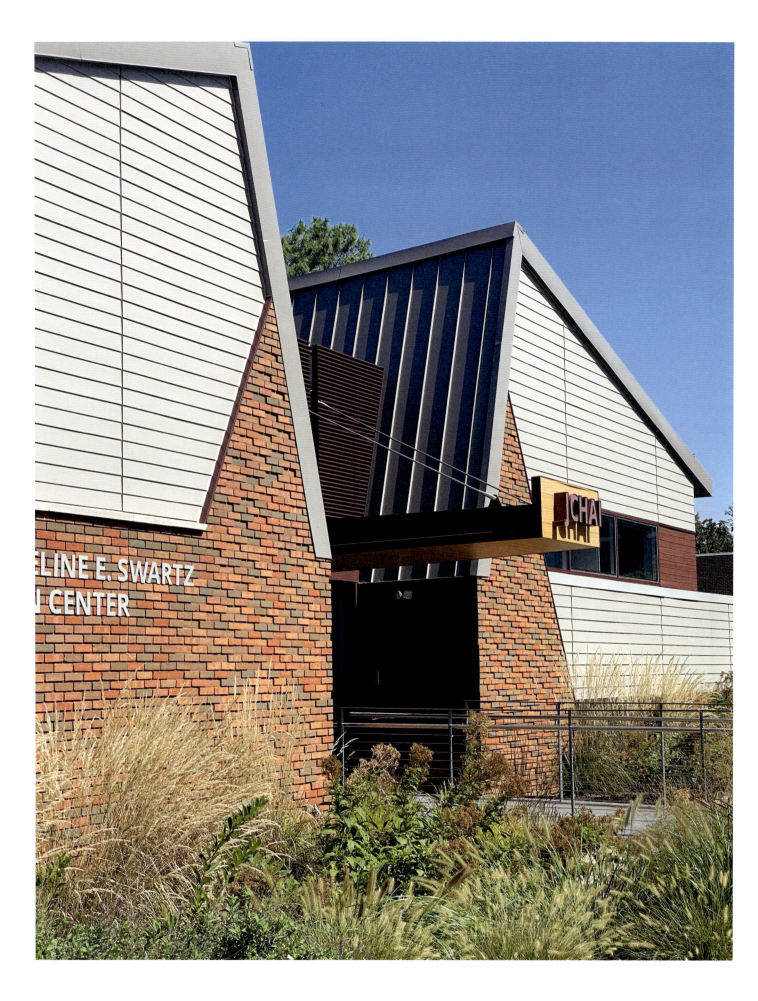

FIRE ENGINE #38

NEW FIRE STATION AND
COMMUNITY HALL IN
HISTORIC DISSTON PARK,
PHILADELPHIA, PA

"Perhaps the best example of both a traditional informal style and bold modern statement is New Engine 38 Fire Station in the City's Tacony section. This stone and brick building with the gable-covered front porch was designed not only to house a city fire brigade but also provide community meeting and function space. And it has to do both while fitting in with its Disston Park surroundings, a feat the building pulled off admirably."

Sandy Smith, *Philadelphia Magazine*

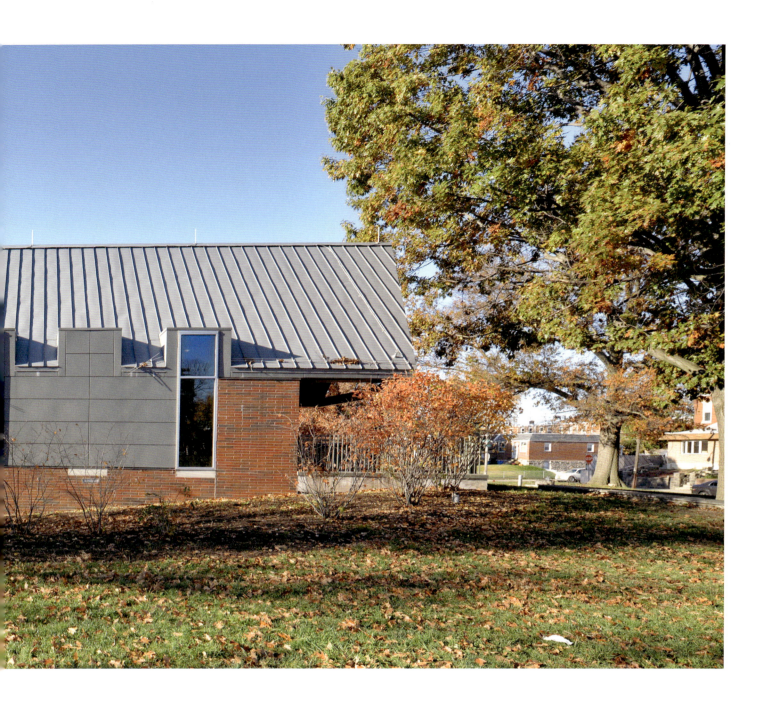

SELECTED WORKSFIRE ENGINE #38335

SELECTED WORKS FIRE ENGINE #38 337

RALSTON/ MERCY-DOUGLASS HOUSE

HUD 202 HOUSING FOR THE ELDERLY WITH AN ADULT HEALTH CENTER, PHILADELPHIA, PA

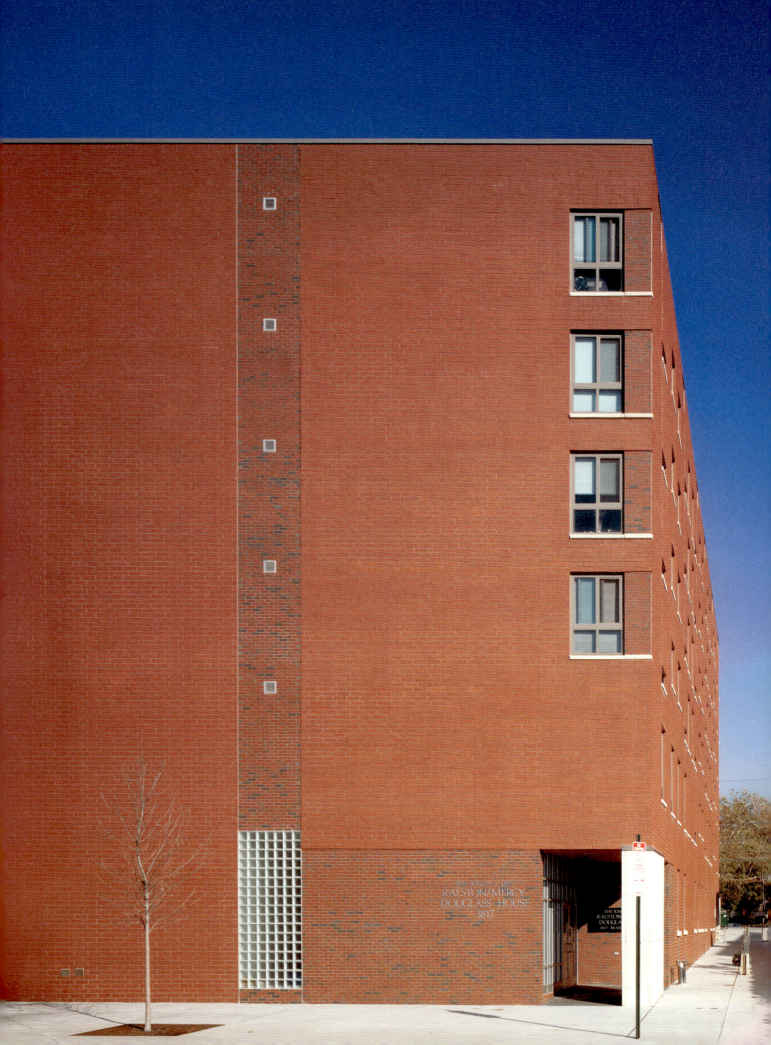

SELECTED WORKS RALSTON/MERCY-DOUGLASS HOUSE 343

ROLLING STOCK HALL

ADDITION TO THE RAILROAD MUSEUM OF PENNSYLVANIA, STRASBURG, PA

"I think this is a very clear thesis. It is carried through right to the very finest details. It does show how a wonderful building can be made through efficient and careful means." AIA Jury

2110 WALNUT STREET

NEW RESIDENTIAL OVERBUILD
WITH ADAPTIVE REUSE OF
HISTORICAL STRUCTURES BELOW,
PHILADELPHIA, PA

SELECTED WORKS 2110 WALNUT STREET

NEW COURTLAND ALLEGHENY CAMPUS

ADULT DAY HEALTH CENTER AND
105 RESIDENTIAL UNITS FOR SENIORS

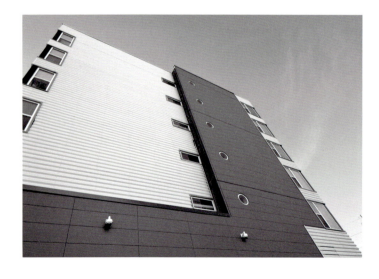

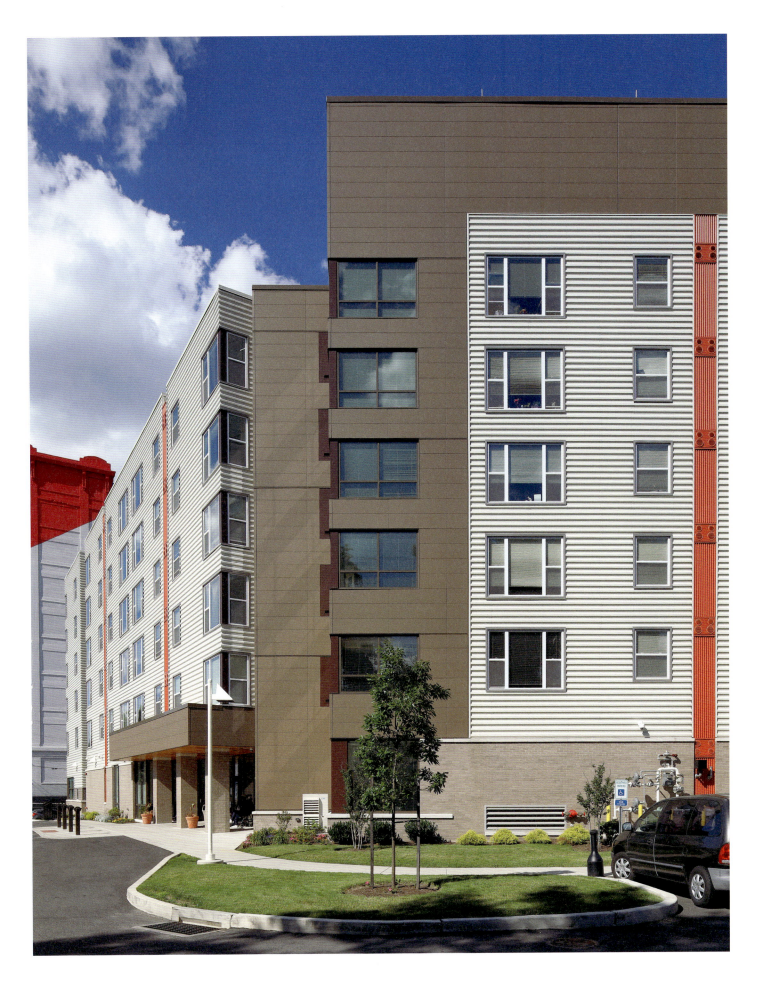

SELECTED WORKS — NEW COURTLAND ALLEGHENY CAMPUS

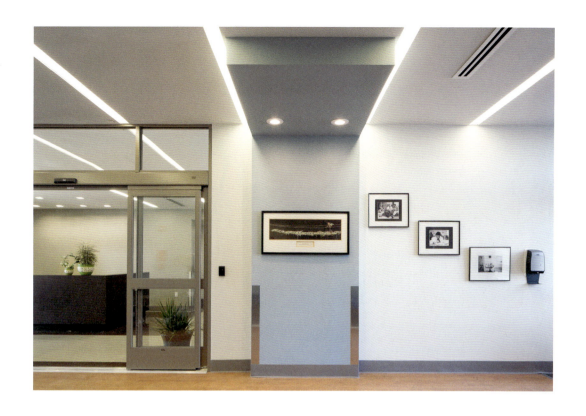

2100 HAMILTON

27 UNIT LUXURY CONDOMINIUM TOWER
ON THE BENJAMIN FRANKLYN PARKWAY,
PHILADELPHIA, PA

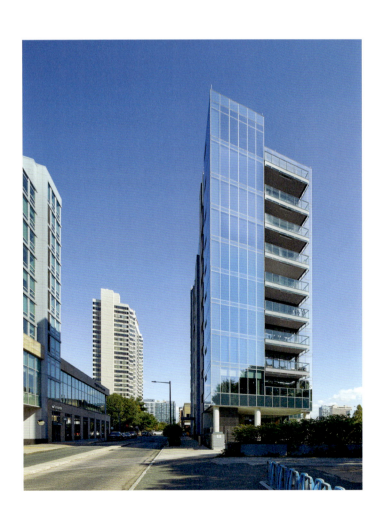

"...overlooking the Parkway. A boulevard not truly understood by Philadelphians. A grand gesture that cleaves the rigid City grid. Often studied, largely maligned, the Parkway is at times a throbbing artery, at other times a setting for memorable celebrations, yet other times a peaceful, tree lined, sun dappled boulevard – the green lung of the City. Much discussed, much studied, the Parkway has confused planners and been judged second class by real estate experts. It is, in fact, beachfront."

Cecil Baker

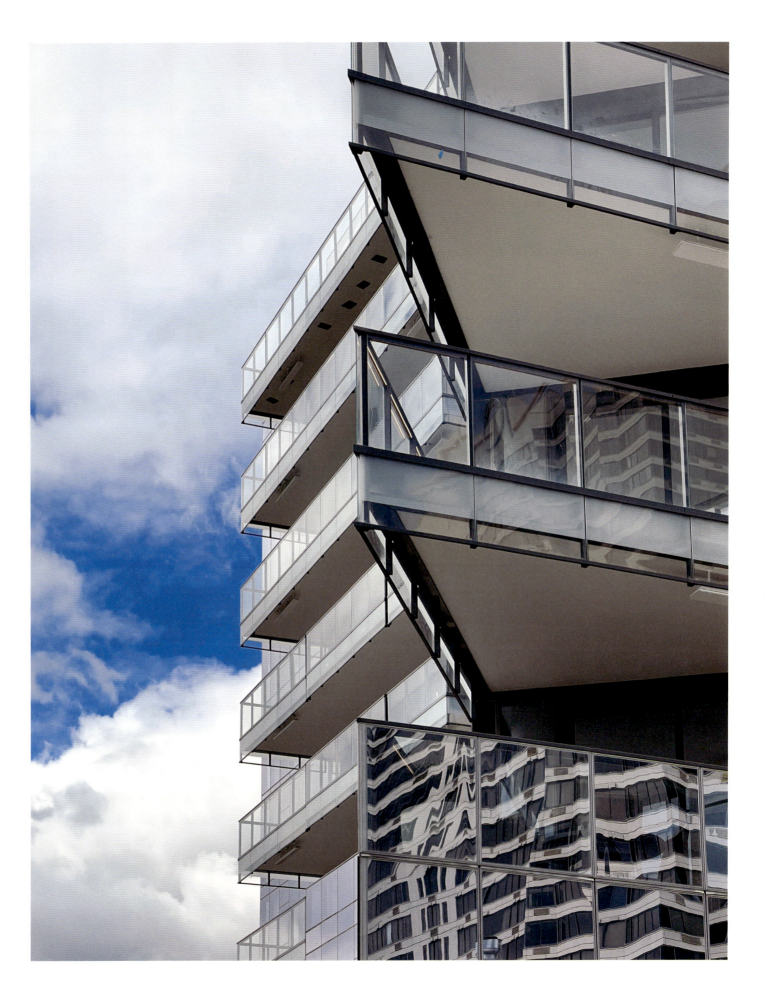

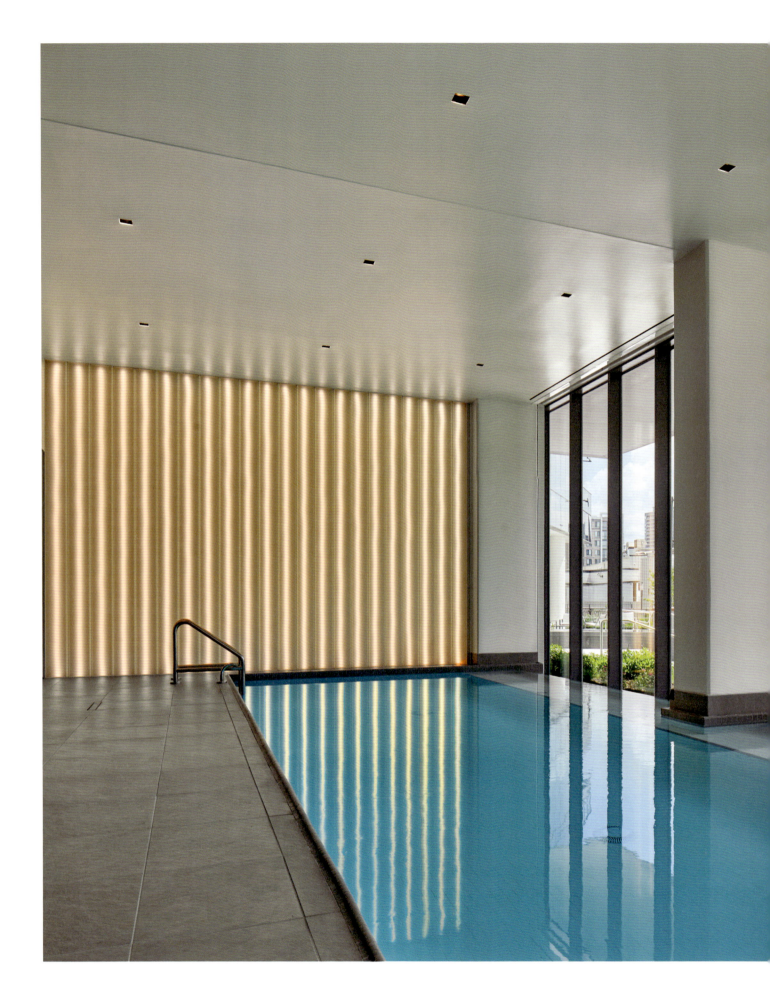

APPENDIX

FINDING MY PLACE

By Cecil Baker

When I was a young boy, my mother and father took me to a house in Mendoza, in the Andes foothills on the western edge of Argentina. Built in the 1930s as a frontier outpost, it was transformed into an artists' salon in the 1920s and frequented by the likes of Jorge Luis Borges. I understood that this place, called Los Alamos, was special. With its vibrant and exotic influences, this Argentine camp house promised shelter yet accepted its arid environment. Overall, I think I responded to its rigorous order, even as I was awed by its sensuality and mystery.

Long after I left Argentina, Los Alamos reverberated in my memory: the simple allocation of spaces inside the fortified wall. The veranda that mediated between the hot, aromatic courtyard and the cool, dark interiors. Place is shaped by culture and myth, weather and time, by the hands of the mason and the carpenter, and sometimes by the whimsy of an architect. Place, in turn, shapes us.

There is also a part of me that resides in Cornwall, Great Britain. There, on Pentyre Headland across from Newquay, is my grandfather's home, Lewinick Cove House. Born in Turkey, Frederick William Baker was a solicitor and financier – and also a gambler who made and lost fortunes. In July 1910, at one of his financial peaks, he bought property and built Lewinick Cove over the next 25 years, interrupted by World War I. Cornish miners carved the cliffs of the jagged shoreline into flat levels to create platforms for his Italianate villa and terraces. The construction crew and many of the building materials were imported from Italy. The curvilinear Romanesque structure clung to the cliffs, hidden from the approach to the entry court. Terraces held a swimming pool and other water features that were replenished by the tides. There was no garden, only a celebration of two abundant local materials, stone and water, with the sea forming a dramatic backdrop.

Lewinick Cove became known as Baker's Folly. Local lore has it that when Frederick was asked why he chose to build such a large, difficult structure on the dank northern inward side of the cove, he answered, "I am Baker."

Lewinick Cove left a lasting impression during a visit early in my career. On approach, one sees nothing below the rim of the headland. A modest cart-way leads to the property's greenhouses and then curves and slices down into the Cornish hillside, culminating in a cliff-lined courtyard and the villa, along with a freestanding tower that served as a guest house. From there an exterior passageway curves along the sea wall, under the overhanging residence, and out to the sunlit ornamental water terraces. Only then does one encounter the home's entryway. Inside, sections of exposed mined rock are visible among the plaster walls, elaborate moldings, and ornate furnishings. Being there was an intense and poetic experience, and it formed a design approach that I later referred to as the choreography of passage.

Beginnings

I am the son of two British parents who made their home in Argentina, not far from Los Alamos, amongst the vineyards and orchards of San Rafael. My father, Hugh Baker, an Eton graduate and Commissioned 2nd Lieutenant in the Royal Horse/Field Artillery, fought in the trenches of northern France from 1915 to 1918. A decorated war hero, he took part in the Battle of the Somme, the Battle of Arras, and the Final Advance in Flanders. After the war my father roamed the world, with postings in Trinidad, Malaysia, and Kenya. His true calling was mining engineering. However, he never found his professional niche. Fate intervened when he followed his father to Argentina. Believing this part of South America to be a rich trove of opportunity, he bought my father a yerba mate plantation in Misiones Province. Thus my father's path was set. He commuted between Nairobi, Kenya, and Concepción De La Sierra, Argentina, for several years.

He met my mother on what was to be his final commute in March 1939, on board the Blue Star Lines Alcantara. Nettie Cook came from a banking family in Anstruther, Scotland, and was on a trip to visit her brother in Argentina. She was 18 years younger than my father, but they fell in love and, after disembarking in Buenos Aires, married and settled on the Misiones plantation.

In 1947, frustrated by President Juan Perón's yerba mate embargo and anti-Anglo hostility, they moved across Argentina to San Rafael, Mendoza.

Farming life was difficult. The local British community made very little attempt to integrate with the locals. Never comfortable with the Spanish language, their communication skills were strained. What's more, the presence of their fellow Europeans – many former Vichy and Nazi expatriates – was awkward to absorb. Thus, I inherited a nuanced sense of belonging. I admired many of my Argentine friends but lived in a home with little sympathy for the local culture. I vividly witnessed my father's anger toward business practices that hinged on "under the table" accommodations. I, on the other hand, admired the Argentinians' freewheeling way of life, with bribery often being an acceptable, even necessary, response to misguided authority. These were the days of Juan Domingo Perón and Evita Duarte. To survive and indeed flourish, one had to find the schisms in the regulations. I took the liberty of applying those lessons even on the school level, and there was much joy within the steps of that tango. Like most of my classmates, I was one precarious step away from being caught and punished for my transgressions.

Some of those reverberating memories have shaped my professional idiosyncrasies. Soon after settling in Mendoza, my mother enrolled my sister and I in a boarding school in La Cumbre, Córdoba, 720 miles from our home. She drove us there, two days across dusty steppes, and deposited us at the foot of the school, perhaps horrified at the enormity of her decision – I was seven, Caroline, six. This was, after all, the only English-speaking school in the region. Mrs Hills' School was not a nurturing institution. It was strict and unforgiving, and the food was particularly challenging. Much of the time I was homesick and terrified, protective of my little sister. But one event brought me to life: I apparently drew a naked man and a naked woman. Mrs. Hills was informed, and as punishment had the staff stitch the two drawings on the back of my blue blazer. Shades of the Scarlett Letter! But with that notoriety came acceptance from my classmates. And most crucially to me, I realized my distinction: I was an artist.

Other formative influences involved my father. He was in his late forties when I was born. Those next years saw him hobbled by one financial failure after another. As his economic resources dwindled, we were perhaps kept afloat by my mother's inheritance.

The early years in San Rafael were particularly devastating, his fledgling orchards and vineyards were beset by untimely frosts, destructive hail storms, and baffling diseases. His failure to assimilate made him an unsympathetic figure in the local community. Ever the Anglo military man – tall, erect, mustached, and dressed in proper British fashion – he was a broad and tempting target. We were all privy to his agony. Mother kept us out of the way.

On returning from school I was immediately put to work. Father relied on me, trusting me with his tractors. I worked from early morning to evening, ploughing, seeding, raking, gathering, and bringing in the harvested grapes and fruit. I took on the responsibility. I learned to be alone. As I sat at the wheel of the tractor or caterpillar, my mind wandered aimlessly, fully at peace. Over my shoulder I would observe the sharp, neat furrow and fanning loam, deriving immense satisfaction from the perfection I was leaving in my wake. To this day, I feel a Zen-like sense of detachment when I am on a tractor.

The cap was not on the gas dispensary
and unhinged
by that simple act of carelessness
his long legs, now
skinny with age,
the madman caromed
across the brown baize
finca looking for the culprit:
that son, recently careless,
hunched loose-boned on the steel parapet of the
caterpillar, yanking one lever, yanking the other, the
yellow nose slapping left, slapping right.
The metallic throb a shelter of noise
within the dusty violence created by the disc
implement.
The engine idled, the dust storm
swept past
and . . .
the startled rabbit paused
and in the wallop of sound that followed the son
perceived his father's face:
blunt jawed, unconditionally pinched as if a
catastrophe of unimaginable consequence was then being
played out:
"How many times have I told you
to make sure that you leave the cap of the gas tank on?"
God, Dad, cool it. It's not that bad
a simple statement over our dinner would do.
Why does my genuine mistake

little mistake, become the vortex of anger that is larger, so much larger, than your rigid body can support?
Let me get this awkward caterpillar in gear again
Clutch, gear, lever
The bright yellow hood leaps forward.

Developing a Vision

After graduating from high school in Buenos Aires, I was sent to the US to become part of the Class of 1963 at Williams College. I was enrolled in a joint program between Williams and MIT whereby one would transfer to MIT at a certain point to become an engineer – a field my family championed as well suited for a responsible son. At Williams, however, I gravitated to the art department. I wanted to be a painter. In my junior year my favorite art instructor, Lee Hirsche, gave me a book on the Mexican architect Luis Barragán: "Look, you can be an artist and an engineer." That moment changed my life: I saw quite clearly that there was a career path for me. I could be an architect, satisfying my parents' practical urgings while enabling me to craft with space, light, and color. From artist to architect. I seldom looked back after this fork in the road.

Perhaps more important, Williams College opened my eyes to the possibility of honesty. I was amazed by the honor system. I no longer had to worry about roaming professors or lurking classroom proctors. There was no reason to break rules, no reason to cheat. I graduated Phi Beta Kappa, deemed Williams' most talented. And while I have always been skittish around clubs, fraternities, and associations because of my resistance to "belonging," I came away from those four formative years with a possible profession and a steady admiration for my new country.

After Williams I enrolled in the architecture program at the University of Pennsylvania. It was the era of the Philadelphia School, peopled by the likes of Louis Kahn, Robert Venturi, and Romaldo Giurgola. Heady days for an aspiring architect in Philadelphia! In my case, however, either because of my mule-like resistance to criticism or the arrogance of the instruction, I did not fit the groove. Louis Kahn was wasted on me. I took a year off to travel Europe and North Africa on a motorcycle and basked in the relief from constraints. This magical trip culminated in my meeting Fairley Ross, the woman who would become my wife and the single greatest influence on

my life, both as a designer and, more important, as a human being. When I returned to the University of Pennsylvania and finished my education, there was only one instructor who pierced my sullen armor: Louis Sauer. A charismatic practitioner, Lou was never a comfortable part of the Graduate School of Architecture, in spite of his remarkable achievements in residential architecture. I learned a lot from Lou Sauer – his passion for order and inventiveness in housing, his tremendous zeal to reinvent the internal geography of residences and the external possibilities of place-making. I saw in him the pure ease of a poet. Most important, Lou allowed my voice into the conversation.

Upon graduation I joined Louis Sauer and Associates and over the next six years worked on a number of assignments, from a single-family home at the New Jersey Shore, to a subsidized residential tower in Bucks County, to a village of twins and townhouses for Wesleyan University. These were largely happy times, though sometimes constrained by periods of national recession, and Lou's office prepared me for my eventual career as a practitioner. The final project I worked on at my mentor's office was Queen Village Mews, an urban cluster of 60 new residential units and 57 rehab units on an open site ringed with industrial architecture. Elliot Rothschild, an associate at the firm and friend of the developer, brought it to the office. Ultimately, for a number of reasons, Elliot and I took the project out of the office and created a new architectural firm: Baker Rothschild Horn and Blyth, including our friends and fellow architects Michael Horn and Alden Blyth in the partnership. Elliot and I submitted Queen Village to the annual Progressive Architecture Awards, sharing the credit with Louis Sauer's office. The P/A Awards recognized risk-taking practitioners and sought to promote progress in the field of architecture. A P/A Award was the most coveted honor in design, and we were thrilled to receive it in 1973 in an awards ceremony at the United Nations complex. While the developer ultimately abandoned the project, it became the springboard for Baker Rothschild Horn and Blyth.

National events soon impinged on the heady launch of our firm. It was 1973, the year of Watergate. The year *Time* magazine ran a cover with the question: "Is the US Going Broke?" By 1974, with the resignation of President Nixon, there was little work for architects, especially in the private residential sector. Like all architects at the time, we faced an uncertain future from our lofty new office at 218 North 13th Street. If Baker Rothschild Horn and Blyth was to survive, we knew we could not wait for projects to come through our door. We'd have to be assertive and creative, take a risk. We'd have to take control of our own future.

A common thread that bound us was our experience rehabilitating our own homes. Out of sheer desperation, we resolved to trade pencils for nail aprons, buy a building shell, and start a construction firm. During the initial years, we four partners performed most of the construction functions, from demolition to carpentry, masonry, and finish trades. Thus, BRHB Developers was born and ultimately evolved into a design firm with an independent construction crew.

The first few years of BRHB Developers were onerous. Whatever we made on a project funded the next project. The four of us lived frugal lives, as our annual incomes were often in the four-figure range. There were no family vacations; our wives saw us unshaven, in construction gear, exhausted by long hours of physical labor. During that period I often questioned my sanity: what was this Ivy League-educated, Louis Kahn disciple doing, banging nails in freezing temperatures, day after day, six days a week?

Nevertheless, the rewards eventually made up for the sacrifices. Over a period of eight years, BRHB developed ten projects totaling 276 residential units and related retail/office space. This included both luxury and subsidized housing, such as Washington Square West Scattered Site Apartments and Dynasty Court, Chinatown – HUD Section 8 projects that came from our reputation as developers of distinctive yet economically efficient buildings. Our work, published here and abroad, played a large part in the resurgence of Philadelphia's Queen Village neighborhood.

Much of what would come to define my aesthetic and philosophy can be found in one of our first built projects, an urban and office complex called Candy Factory Court that emerged in the mid-1970s. There was nothing easy about this formative project. Zoning mandated residential use, and the old structure was severely compromised. The only open space was a narrow inset between two of the three structures that had been joined to form the 15,000 square-foot factory. And the recession cast a long shadow. But we had faith that we could turn the old candy factory into something vital and new. We did this by carving out light wells, gardens, and interior courtyards

along the wide, column-less spaces, transforming the project into a desirable cluster of unique homes and offices. We fully believed we could honor the history of the abandoned building while awakening a dormant part of Philadelphia. This required negotiating with a community and zoning board that was wary of mixed-use development. We spent a year and a half with sawdust in our hair, and when it was done, Candy Factory Court wasn't just a financial success and a model for much of what subsequently occurred in Queen Village, it was also published around the world and recognized with regional and national awards. Candy Factory Court is an early example of adaptive reuse and was the foundation of my practicality. I call it spending money on the sunny side of the drywall. One architectural critic called me the "poet of the prosaic." I couldn't ask for more.

"From forlorn (Candy) factory to exceptional dwellings."

"The spectacular well space, filled with daylight from skylights in the roof, gives the design a drama and verticality seldom achieved in residential design."

"What was once a long-abandoned eyesore has now been converted into four townhouses that make the most of the industrial elements of this former candy factory, creating exciting modern living spaces that also maintain the historic fabric of this urban neighborhood."

"The spectacular well space, filled with daylight from skylights in the roof, gives the design a drama and verticality seldom achieved in residential design."
Architectural Record, Record Houses of 1979

BRHB Developers spent more than $30 million reinvigorating the city, largely focusing on the forgotten industrial corridors that today are some of its most desirable real estate assets:

Queen Village Mews: 13 bi-level condominium units
Hanson Square: 37 new townhouses
Catharine Commons: 7 luxury condominiums
Passyunk Row: 9 condominium apartments and four build-to-suit residences
Candy Factory Court: 4 build-to-suit residences and 8,000 sf of rental office space
Washington Square West Scattered Site Apartments: 135 HUD Section 8 units.
Mattress Factory: 6 luxury loft apartments and 4 build-to-suit residences
Dynasty Court: 56 HUD Section 8 apartments and 8,000 sf of retail space

Lombard Mews: 6 new custom residences

Most critically for me, the income these projects generated in later years permitted me to think of my return to my chosen profession as a hobby.

By the late 1970s, Baker Rothschild Horn and Blyth was in full swing, designing for other developers as well as our own projects. We broadened our marketing goals in the architectural practice, and soon, largely due to Michael and Elliot's skillful salesmanship, had projects for the City of Philadelphia, the Department of General Services of the State of Pennsylvania, the General Services Administration, and the Department of Defense. Meanwhile, I pursued the residential developer client base and the single-family housing market.

In 1982, a national architecture and planning firm approached us to ask about forming a joint venture that would combine their planning capabilities with our development and architecture experience. While working out the details of this marriage, my inner "wise facilitator" reminded me of my original craving to be an artist/architect. The joint venture was eventually scuttled and I veered off to form Cecil Baker and Associates.

BRHB Developers, however, fundamentally made me who I am today: an architect who has the innate tools of a builder/developer. It opened my eyes to see opportunity in derelict urban settings and dormant industrial complexes. At various times in my career I crafted the solutions and then chose the development entity to develop the vision. This hands-on knowledge also led me to be part of transformative projects such as Turning on the Lights Upstairs, an urban intervention that arguably was instrumental in bringing significant change to Philadelphia.

In April 1982 I launched Cecil Baker and Associates with a few architectural assignments from "angel" clients. I could not have done it otherwise. Our office at 105 South 12th Street was a six-story building owned by a client and friend, Howard Winig. Howard provided the "white box" – a conference room and two partially enclosed offices. Jim Wolters, Kate Cleveland, Bill Cheeseman, Kevin Blackney, and Shep Houstoun followed me from BRHB to Cecil Baker & Partners. By 1983 we were fully launched. Once again we found ourselves in the teeth of a major economic recession, but it was manageable due to the reliable income from Paul Weinberg, our most significant client, for

whom we had office projects in Allentown, Pennsylvania; Raleigh, North Carolina; and Austin, Texas. When the private sector faltered, I followed my contacts in the public sector. Other key contributors to our fledgling enterprise included Center in the Park, Diamond Park Housing, Hertz Turnaround Facility at Philadelphia International Airport, the Intercultural Center at the University of Pennsylvania, and Temple University Medical Offices. When work was slow, John Howard, newly hired, coached us in Computer Aided Design (CAD), using the West Chester University Dorms project as the platform for change. We survived, but just barely. Those years tested the limits of my endurance, but I was blessed with amazing co-workers. I know it's not easy to work for a boss who hogs the design process and is private and uncommunicative. Nevertheless, we had an amazing team.

Nancy Bastian joined the firm in 1984, Eric Leighton in 2000. In 2007, Nancy and Eric were made partners. We changed our name to Cecil Baker + Partners and moved to 1107 Walnut Street. Chris Blakelock, who had been with us since 1998, became a partner in 2013 but had to withdraw for medical reasons in 2019. For more than 17 years, Nancy, Eric, and Chris were instrumental in making the firm what it is today. Nancy took over the financial reins and most of the management. Eric managed the larger, more complex projects, such as 500 Walnut, Western Union Condominiums, and much of the public city work. Nancy took my clients in the public sector and developed our portfolio in the social service and subsidized housing sector, ultimately developing her own client base.

At the end of 2022 I withdrew from the firm to pursue a few bespoke architectural projects and revisit my original passion: sketching and painting. During that period, in the aftermath of the pandemic, I had a hard time going to a largely empty office. I came to realize how much I appreciated the serendipity that occurs in a cluster of individuals pursuing a common goal of excellence. Letting go was a difficult transition, but I came to acknowledge that it had to happen. Nancy and Eric will take the new firm, CBP Architects, in their own design direction, free of the demanding and arbitrary old boss. Bless them!

Design Philosophy

When I look back over the body of my work at Baker Rothschild Horn and Blyth, Cecil Baker & Associates, and Cecil Baker + Partners – the Partners – the private houses, residential villages and high-rises, homes for challenged populations, civic and institutional buildings – I am reminded of the many influences that have shaped and defined my architecture, the memories that have come into play, the persuasions of art and nature. I see my constant fascination with affinities, order, and meaning. I see a steady respect for context and environment. I see buildings that yearn to be entered into and remembered, to live on as an echo over time.

When I am asked who my mentors are, I offer the following names: Louis Barragán, Andy Goldsworthy, and Edouard Vuillard.

Barragán for the:
- Staging of quiet harmonious space
- Celebration of silence
- Splendor of order
- Equilibrium - nature and the architect's intervention

Goldsworthy for the:
- The overwhelming power of nature
- Ideas of growth, perpetual change, transformation

Vuillard for the:
- Instilling of poetic meaning in the everyday
- Interplay of tone and color, explicit yet mysterious
- Sophistication in creating visual depth

The Persuasion of Place

Shortly after leaving Williams College, I studied a book called *Architecture Without Architects*. I was amazed by the potential of buildings to express the climate around them, sometimes in flamboyant ways. I fully endorse architectural mannerisms that express the local and regional rhythms of nature. I believe that sustainable initiatives will lead us into a fuller expression of regional architecture through buildings that use local materials, respond directly to environmental concerns, and poetically express the particulars of natural light and local building traditions. We open our hearts and buildings to nature. Context directs and ordains.

Architects design within regulatory frameworks, be they local, regional, or national. I believe it is critical to understand the intention of the legislation as well as the community's practical concerns. Moreover, we have a responsibility to look at the broad dynamics and act wisely, often independently. No building exists in a vacuum. We are citizens of the

environment, landscape, and community. We live in a highly complex, interrelated world. When the US sneezes, Argentina catches a cold.

Living and working in Philadelphia, I have absorbed the dominant Colonial strands of history. I take these basic paradigms and rearrange them to create a more abstract, less particular grid. Once I have found "my" grid I will allow an occasional surprise to make the calming symmetry jump its tracks. A hint of an abstract cornice, lintel, or sill may appear randomly within the organizing grid. The demarcation between residential elements might wander from its logical place. My work in formerly industrial neighborhoods also reinterprets their heritage, assuming the industrial muscularity while also skewing its relentless purposefulness. My taller buildings relate, albeit abstractly, to the lower-scale residential, commercial, or institutional setting at their base, then grow freely skyward, rejoicing in an abstract lexicon. This is how I fit in.

The Power of Simple Shapes

Architecture is the art that is most affected by the abundant realities of everyday life. I am interested in the simple shapes from childhood – the square, the circle, the triangle. These, I think, have the power to lift us above the complexities, contradictions, and superfluous clutter of our lives. Simplicity has the potential to resolve the visual chaos around us. Simplicity brings with it monumentality and those fundamental architectural concepts of compression and release, enclosure and transparency.

Simplicity gifts us with lucid moments in time: if a question is not asked, the need for an answer does not exist. We need to be able to create moments for reflection, for the murmurings of change, for potential transformation.

For me, design is a choice of what to leave out, rather than what to put in. I have grown to love blank walls; they are the parenthesis for planned turbulence. To me, there is nothing like a moment of wonder in which I can digest the inevitable complexities that will greet me on the other side.

Once the simple shapes are comprehended, it is the crevices and cracks that will allow the light to shine through. Simple shapes are the lanterns of my landscape, the reward for coming out of the hail storm. They are the beacons that temporarily signify tranquility and welcome the murmured mantra. Serene high-performance architecture.

The joy of the simple and obvious!

The Choreography of Passage

I have always believed that good architecture is like a book – each chapter opens the promise of the next, and the plot remains incomplete until the last page. There's a restlessness in that – a purposeful restlessness, a graceful restlessness. There's a tension between the building and the person walking through. I am in pursuit of quiet theater. I seek to create spaces that beckon and suggest mystery, that remain in the mind after the last space has been visited. Among the tools I use to craft the journey are:

Space modulation. When we envision the volume of an enclosure, our palette consists of a floor, walls, and ceiling. In the past, designers would routinely modulate passage with assertive floor plane shifts. In today's world, because we are sensitive to mobility challenged fellow travelers, floors play a restricted role in defining volume changes, largely through material or texture. However, because of their very flatness, floors retain the virtue of being able to blur transitions, particularly inviting the outside in, and vice versa. Walls remain a rich trove of architectural possibilities through their qualities of assertiveness, transparency, and texture. Alone or paired, they are limitless in staking out passage. Ceilings, then, have taken on the rich burden of defining volume. Just as blank walls help usher powerful thresholds, purposely dropped or raised ceilings enable us to craft those precious moments of suspense as a prelude to release.

My vision is that, as we walk through architecture, we momentarily lock in the scene in front of us. We move from one threshold to the next, like flipping cards in a rolodex. Each one distinct, it's information cataloging itself. I ask the traveller to make sense of it. I ask the traveller to be a participant in assembling the passage. If I provide clues, but not the answer, then I have succeeded.

Symmetry/Asymmetry. Symmetry is an artificial construct, but it has the benefit of suggesting completion and mental tranquility. It is, purposely, a temporary point of equilibrium. To move forward, however, an insistent grain of asymmetry must intrude. When symmetry is toppled and the thrust of a new direction dominates,

that moment is a powerful, muscular occasion. It is a beautiful stage in architecture where the storyteller comes on stage. I look to integrate the formal with the informal, the symmetrical with the asymmetrical, seeking orderliness, grace and dignity.

When confronted with corners, the stitching together of simple shapes, interior or exterior, I emphasize that they are the strongest sinew in our arsenal of design interventions. They are the hinge to harmony. It is in the corners that the story is told. They represent that purposeful realignment that connects one chapter to the next: they are the byline.

The Shared Exploration

Every project begins with a conversation. Every conversation deepens, and in turn deepens trust as the architect and client develop a commonality of dream and language. The longer I practice architecture, the more I come to see the power of collaboration and kinship, the good that comes from sitting down and actively listening to what the client says.

But it has taken me a long time to truly come to terms with who I am as an architect and how I must engage with my clients. At times, frankly, I have been reluctant to know myself. At times, I have discovered things about myself by listening to the life stories of others.

I am concerned with the rich trove of possibilities in architecture. These things live in me quite wholly. But I have tended to be private about these concerns, for as passionate as I am about what I do and why, I am ultimately a shy person. When asked about my beliefs, I have, in the past, found myself growing stingy, even angry. Perhaps I have come across as aloof or judgmental. This kind of waffling around philosophy doesn't help an architect and it doesn't sustain a business. Clients have said, "Cecil, I like your work, but I am left wondering where you are in it. I don't know what you stand for."

How tempted I have been to sweep design in behind their backs.

But owners, whether private or corporate or institutional, are people. My clients want their buildings to be unique, but they don't want to look like fools. Ideally, I must serve as a safe shepherd to create a building that is original for them, that makes them proud and stretches them to new possibilities. To do

that, I have to partner with them, do I not? I have to know them. I have to be interested in who they are.

Design Philosophy

The Persuasion of Place. The Power of Simple Shapes. The Choreography of Passage. The Shared Exploration. These four tenets are my guideposts in the pursuit of cohesive, peaceful, well-considered, and memorable architecture. I sum them up in my statement of philosophy:

Inclusion Informs Form

This is arguably an overly cute pairing of words. However, the phrase has meaning for me, and I explain it as follows:

Many sculptors have a vision and then chip away at their block of marble to translate their idea into something tangible, palpable.

I do not approach my projects with a vision. Instead, I look to the marble for its secrets. I have always been an architect who looks for the chinks in the block of marble for clues as to where to first place my chisel. Before I put pencil to paper, I want to know everything there is to know about my project.

My pencil then leads me who knows where. I follow. Integration, inclusion, harmony – guided by these principles, I have found my place.

A solo architect?
Tan poco does it seem –
what is it?
All alone.
Change is changing
all the time
continue usted por favor
no me dejes aqui atras.
En cambiando me cambio
de aqui hasta alla.
Y los que dejo por detras
I will leave them there
It's unfortunate we suppose
that you caught me here
bilingual
lastima que en mi cambio
you, who are quite decent,
catapulted into prominence
como simbolo de my pasado
imperfect
now see my graceless exit

CLIENTS & HEROES

By Cecil Baker

As I look back at my career I see that there are six clients who have had an outsized impact on my design beliefs. They helped me define myself, imbued me with courage, and were loyal and supremely supportive. What's more, they helped me become a better citizen of the US, and of Philadelphia in particular.

Paul Weinberg, Landmark Associates/Connaught Corporation, for whom Cecil Baker & Associates completed offices in Allentown, Pennsylvania; Raleigh, North Carolina; and Austin, Texas. He was introduced to us by Ed Boyer, the husband of Olivier Dunrea, who was our secretary/office manager at Baker Rothschild Horn and Blyth. Ed Boyer was then working for John Rahenkamp, fellow faculty with Louis Sauer at Penn, and like Lou was a talented outlier at the Penn Graduate School of Design.

Paul was modest in his own personal habits but took enormous risks in entering new markets across the US, on the basis of academic research by Bernard Mennis, a professor at Temple University's Department of Political Science. Paul wished to be a leader in the speculative office market in second-tier cities with perceived growth potential and demonstrable quality-of-life credentials. He was always willing to test new design paradigms, including sustainable practices that incorporated pioneer engineering studies coming out of the Princeton Energy Group (these were the days of the 1970s energy crisis).

Paul Weinberg's firm retained Cecil Baker & Associates for a number of office projects:

Commerce Plaza II and Commerce Plaza III, Allentown, Pennsylvania, comprise 160,000 square feet of speculative office space on a 48-acre site at the intersection of the Northeast Extension of the Pennsylvania Turnpike, Route 22 and I-78. Completed in 1985.

Metro Park, a 100,000-square-foot speculative office in the dynamic Research Triangle Region of Raleigh, NC. Fully leased to IBM before completion in 1984.

Great Hills I, II, and III: a 21-acre site fronting on a major arterial loop in Austin, Texas. Completed in 1988. The design challenge was to place 197,000

APPENDIX

square feet of office space in a steep, densely wooded setting without significantly destroying the very characteristics that made the site unique. Paul Weinberg wanted a design that would clearly set his project apart from the ubiquitous dark-glass boxes and postmodern derivations that increasingly dotted the western hills of Austin.

The site slopes to the southwest, providing views across the hills toward Austin. The buildings are placed on the mid-ground of the site to use the slope to maximum advantage. The choice allows for upper and lower entrances, each with contiguous parking. The parking is loosely worked into the slopes to retain as many trees as possible.

The building's shape – a gentle curve broken by a parallelogram – was generated from the site's contours, solar considerations, and the view orientation. The major curved form responds to the undulating hills. The parallelogram sweeps through the curve to accentuate the entry points and maximize the views toward Austin. In a climate where air-conditioning is used year-round, the client wanted to limit solar gain but maximize natural daylighting. To that end, the Princeton Energy Group became part of the design team – the design was modeled and a series of green strategies were implemented:

- The western face of the parallelogram is deeply carved to avoid heat gain from the afternoon summer sun.
- The southern fenestration incorporates horizontal windows divided into two bands. The upper band uses clear glass with scalloped screening to maximize light penetration deep into the office space, while the lower band of glass is tinted to reduce solar gain. This also allows office workers full views to the outside.
- The northern facades view are fully glazed to maximize daylighting.
- The interior atrium incorporates the lower and upper entries into a changing dynamic that reflects the exterior architecture and is exclusively lit with north-facing clerestories.
- The office building incorporates Building Management Systems.
- The office complex includes ice storage systems below grade. This strategy permitted downsizing of the AC systems normally designed for a hypothetical peak summer load.
- The landscape design preserved mature juniper and live oak species and incorporated swales for water

retention. The three buildings, along with site walls made of dry limestone harvested from the property, help to navigate the grade changes.

The design, I believe, reflects harmony within the eco-system, the site, the regulatory framework, the program, the choices of systems and materials, and Paul Weinberg's aspirations.

Paul Weinberg withdrew from the world of real estate development at the completion of Great Hills III. I have not heard from him since, though I was told that he had moved to Paris to write scripts for theater productions. This is may be an apocryphal story. But I miss Paul; his courage and decency were inspiring. He afforded me unconstrained design opportunities and surrounded himself, and us, with the best and the brightest. He was fun to work for!

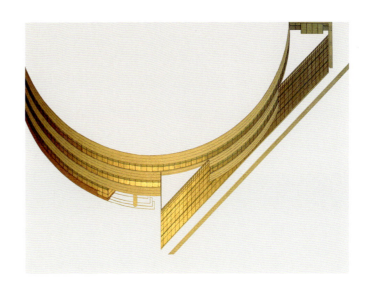

Ted Robb, Regional Administrator for HUD, was a partner of BRHB Developers on the Dynasty Court Section 8 project, and a subsequent client of Cecil Baker & Associates for his own project in Northern Liberties – Neumann Senior Housing. Here is an excerpt describing the project from his autobiography:

". . . I learned that the buildings in question dated to 1898 and 1915 and included about 70,000 square feet. I was very hesitant to take on the project, especially after I visited. As I suspected, the building's architecture was absolutely beautiful. To convert it into low-income housing would cost a fortune. This would be the largest project I had overseen . . .

"Nevertheless, I contacted architect Cecil Baker, a veteran of HUD work whom I had worked with before. He and I spent two nights in sleeping bags camping out in the old abandoned hospital as we thought about what we could do. It was kind of eerie.

"The property is a historic preservationist's dream. Cast iron balustrades decorate columned porches that reach four stories high. Most of the exterior materials—brick, limestone, granite, and terracotta—needed restoration. Inside, painted murals decorate the walls, beautifully complementing stained-glass illustrations that pop up everywhere. In addition to two elevators, a restored grand staircase connects the building's five floors. Most rooms have floor-to-ceiling bay windows, and quite a few have roof terraces. Interior units look down on a lovely private courtyard. The property's crown jewel, though, is a domed chapel decorated with ornate stained-glass windows.

"After my initial hesitation, I fell in love with the building. Cecil and I envisioned that it could hold sixty-nine one-bedroom units for low-income senior citizens. We planned for a large community room on the third floor, and Cecil designed each of the residential floors to have its own lounge and living room area.

"Nearly seventeen years after work began in 2004, it is a true joy to walk around Neumann Senior Housing, especially when I am feeling low. The chapel brings me such serenity. Before the pandemic, I took prayers and conversations with my guardian angel there." **The Other Side of this Life**, Ted Robb, Luminare Press

"Ted Robb opened Neumann Senior Housing last month with 69 subsidized one-bedroom apartments. The residence, converted by Cecil Baker & Associates, may be the least antiseptic project ever financed by the US Department of Housing and Urban Development in Philadelphia." Changing Skyline, Inga Saffron, *Philadelphia Inquirer*, 2016.

Ted Robb inspired and coached me to seek design fulfillment within the world of affordable housing. His place in my legacy was further reinforced when he introduced Cecil Baker & Associates to Roy Diamond and Joe Sherrick, who provide affordable housing development advisory services to a broad clientele of not-for-profit institutions and re-developers across the Pennsylvania region. Roy and Joe ushered our firm into multiple exciting affordable housing projects including residential projects for Inglis House, NewCourtland, Northern Home for Children, Catholic Housing and Community Services, Hope PHL and others. All in all, more than 1,000 built affordable units.

Jay Cranmer, MCW Properties, former founding partner of Lincoln Properties, which was to become the largest real estate development entity in the US, with projects nationwide. Jerry Cope, partner in Cope Linder Architects, introduced us.

As a result of my development experience I had set my sights on the Lippincott Building in Philadelphia's Washington Square West. The former publishing house sits on the east side of the square in the Society Hill neighborhood. J. B. Lippincott was the oldest manufacturing house in the US and published historical, biographical, and standard medical and technical books, including Worcester's Academic Dictionary, Chambers's Encyclopedia, Lippincott's Pronouncing Gazetteer of the World, Lippincott's Pronouncing Biographical Dictionary, and Lippincott's Monthly Magazine.

Changes in the fortunes of technical publishing companies, however, ultimately forced the owner to abandon the five-story masonry, steel, and heavy timber building. It was used for offices in the last decade before sitting empty for a good number of years. How could a building with so much historical heft – and a prominent park side location – lie dormant and unattended?

Center City's residential resurgence suggested the potential for a reborn Lippincott Building. Its adaptive reuse as residential units, however, confronted one substantial problem. The acquisition price, set by its European owners, had been inflexibly established at book value and was sufficiently high to discourage residential developers. To make the project financially feasible, I conceived of creating new real estate on the roof (recognizing that the base building had originally been designed and engineered for seven floors of mill use and was therefore probably overbuilt for residential loads). Working with the Philadelphia Historical Commission, we proposed a rooftop addition held within a 33-degree angle of the parapet. The elongated pyramid, thus defined, became the area within which the expansion could take place.

I pitched the idea to Jay Cranmer, a national developer with a proven record of delivering quality projects in difficult urban settings. He intuitively saw the value, adding his own assessment of the appropriate development scenario. The adaptive reuse project preserved the Lippincott Building's distinct architectural presence by fitting twenty-three condominium apartments within the existing structure and retaining all window and door openings. The residences range in size from 1,500 square feet to 4,500 square feet.

The roof addition incorporates three two-story townhouse penthouses. The new penthouse construction is set back from the existing parapet on all sides to remain well within the pyramid agreed to by the Philadelphia Historical Commission. In addition to preserving sight lines around the building, this setback allowed for the creation of continuous garden terraces.

The Lippincott Building was completed in 2010. Thanks to MCW Properties, one of Philadelphia's architectural treasures is once again contributing to the vitality of Washington Square. Moreover, the Lippincott Building offers visible proof of the adaptability of our historic heritage. It has become one of Philadelphia's premier addresses. It also ushered in a new prototype in the residential market: raw space delivered within a finished framework, with each new condo owner entitled to custom-designed living quarters.

Jay Cranmer subsequently retained Cecil Baker & Associates to design three significant residential projects across the river from Philadelphia:

- Bishop's View, a luxury rental townhome community consisting of 200 residences built on a 9-acre site fronting the Cooper River in Cherry Hill, New Jersey.
- Brook View, a gated community of 116 luxury rental apartments on 15.5 acres in suburban Evesham Township, New Jersey.
- Burrough's Mill, a 308-unit gated luxury rental community on a 26-acre site adjacent to a woodland preserve in suburban Cherry Hill, New Jersey.

Paul Levy, founding president and CEO of the Philadelphia Center City District (CCD), a private-sector-sponsored municipal authority chartered to provide supplemental services that make Philadelphia's downtown commercial area clean, safe, and attractive.

Paul was a friend from Queen Village who retained Cecil Baker & Associates to investigate the accelerating vacancy rates in the upper floors of Philadelphia's older commercial buildings. Notably, its mission was to go beyond the scope of most urban planning investigations by including steps to stimulate their renovation and reuse. We were the lead consultant and worked with a voluntary advisory group of real estate developers, city officials, and the CCD. The resulting 1996 report, titled "Turning on the Lights Upstairs," served as a guide for converting upper floors of older commercial buildings for residential use.

The study methodology involved meeting with the owners, surveying and drawing up the properties, and producing alternate development scenarios (residential vs. commercial). The Department of Licenses and Inspections was consulted to develop a safety score system for each building where elements such as fire ratings, egress lighting, detectors, and alarm systems were weighed against costlier alternatives such as additional fire stairs and sprinkler systems.

The CCD met with the Philadelphia Building and Trades Council to secure support in establishing a "demonstration program" for initial projects to contain renovation costs.

The CCD emerged with strong commitments from local financial institutions to earmark combined construction and permanent financing vehicles for a number of demonstration projects.

The CCD formed a development consultant team to assist current owners in establishing viable development pro formas, including building surveys, schematic designs, estimated costings, and help in obtaining financing.

As a result of the study, City Council passed favorable tax legislation to further encourage building converters. Today many office/retail structures have been converted to residential use under the umbrella of the Tax Abatement Act, becoming the catalyst for thousands of new urban condominium units.

Co-authors: Center City District (Paul Levy, Executive Director, and Nancy Goldenberg, Project Manager); Development Advisor: Gene LeFevre

"Thoughtful research of the problem of vacant and underutilized commercial space in older urban Center City, Philadelphia. Provides a valuable handbook for building owners interested in finding new uses for vacant upper floors in their buildings." AIA Awards Jury.

After Turning on the Lights Upstairs was complete in 1996, Paul retained me as an advisor on architectural strategies to foster development on the Reading Viaduct, as well as to partner with Paul and Laurie Olin on possible urban strategies to encourage development on the Parkway in Philadelphia.

Paul Levy is one of my heroes. Within the context of my community, no one has fought harder to offer the possibility of change. He has succeeded on many urban planning interventions, and Philadelphia is radically the better for it. He has also, painfully, I imagine, seen much of his brilliant leadership thwarted by parochial and political short-sightedness.

I have two parallel heroes: Inga Saffron, the Pulitzer Prize–winning architectural critic for the Philadelphia Inquirer; and Rick Gross, president of the Center City Residents Association (CCRA). Inga's articles on urban and architectural projects are always honest and invite us to consider tolerant and progressive alternatives to traditional urban development. Rick, recently retired from the CCRA, was tireless in championing the resurgence of our city, which was hobbled by the ugly cobwebs of the pandemic. I worked with Rick on an urban task force to interface with the owners of two major developments in the Rittenhouse area of Philadelphia. The mission was to make their large city interventions more neighborhood friendly while keeping the process free of legal bickering.

They are my Three Musketeers: Paul, Inga, and Rick have been, in my lifetime, the gatekeepers to the heathens at our door!

Tom Scannapieco, Scannapieco Development

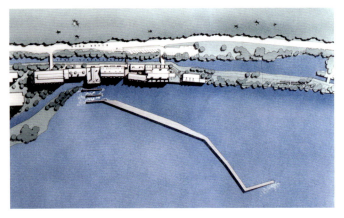

My BRHB experience led me to explore the tremendous development opportunity at the Waterworks, New Hope, Pennsylvania – a thin strand of industrial architecture fronting a dramatic wing dam on the Delaware River in a thriving artists' community. Cecil Baker & Associates provided feasibility studies for various development entities assessing the viability of adaptive reuse. Some saw the value of hydro-electric power, others the economic opportunities in an arts-related facility. No one, however, had a financeable plan.

The site is a slender, 10-acre tract created by the Delaware River and the Pennsylvania Canal. It had accommodated various mills since the 1820s; the wing dam and water wheel were constructed in 1831 to harness the water's energy. Union Mill Paper Company first began building on the site in the 1880s, adding structures to meet growing demand until the company ceased operations in 1971. The abandoned mill comprised a string of seven contiguous and two freestanding structures. Since 1971, the abandoned mill had suffered two major fires and was well on its way to full collapse.

Then along came Tom Scannapieco, a developer with a vibrant history of adaptive reuse in Philadelphia's struggling neighborhoods. Attracted by the mill's marketable location and spectacular views, he retained our firm to explore development possibilities for the complex. The site's constraints presented a challenging design problem that was compounded by difficult zoning issues and a borough that previous developers had repeatedly abandoned at the altar. The island is subject to sporadic flooding (the site is 100 percent in the floodway), offers extremely limited on-site parking, and is accessible only from four canal-side, one-lane historic bridges.

In order to a) meet the parking requirements for residential development, and b) take every unit out of the flood plain, the first and most basic decision was to put the cars within the building. This solved the parking and access problem by establishing a one-way traffic pattern, entering at one end of the complex and exiting at the other. That solution also put every unit at least 8 feet above grade and thus clear of the 100-year-flood elevation. That meant, however, that fully one third of the mill's space was devoted to a low use (parking). To offset the loss of rentable units, we knew we had to add real estate. We expanded the existing structures upward on the river side to the ridge, keeping the canal side true to its historic pedigree. The Waterworks's 62 units have layouts as varied as the stock into which they were designed, reinforcing the mill's lively eclecticism.

". . . a remarkable hundred-year case study of Bucks County mill architecture . . . the architects satisfied the borough's desire to retain a sense of antiquity while providing the developer a highly marketable housing complex."

"Fitting the Waterworks complex into the footprint of the old mill buildings produced a remarkably broad range of building types and unit configurations, which aided the developer in marketing the project." Architectural Record, July 1990

A few years after the Waterworks was completed, I ran into Tom Scannapieco at a book signing. I invited him to look at plans and elevations that my office had prepared for 500 Walnut Street, directly behind Independence Hall, for other local and national developers. Tom took one look at the architectural renderings and immediately saw the promise of a unique project. He never looked back.

Independence National Historical Park was radically reconfigured in 2008. One of the most controversial revisions resulting from the National Park Service (NPS) and Olin Studio design was the relocation of the Liberty Bell pavilion from a central location to its current location on the park's western perimeter. The wisdom behind this change was to enable the viewer to see open sky above and to each side of the Independence Hall cupola when standing directly behind the Liberty Bell.

When Penn Mutual Insurance Company decided to sell open ground to the east of its 26-story headquarters complex, that piece of real estate lay squarely within the view-shed that NPS assumed would be open in perpetuity behind Independence Hall.

In the ensuing years, local and national developers sketched designs for a number of uses. Ultimately, they all walked away from the project because of the uneconomical floor plate resulting from required setbacks from the adjoining Penn Mutual tower and the receding profile dictated by the NPS view corridor.

However, Tom saw an opportunity to create a unique residential structure large enough to deliver one or two luxury units per floor. Aimed at the very apex of the residential market, this slender needle tower would house units of 6,000 square feet or less per floor and offer unparalleled views of Philadelphia and its historic heritage. These customizable homes in the sky would be on the threshold of the most sacred 51 acres in America.

Our architectural mission was to satisfy NPS requirements while maximizing the park frontage. The municipality capped the height of new buildings on Walnut Street's southern side at 45 feet and required a 25-foot setback from the vertical plane of the property line – hence the shape of 500 Walnut Street. For their part, the Society Hill Civic Association had long feared contemporary intrusions in their historic neighborhood. We secured their approval by pulling the building back from St. James Street (the northern cobbled street); by placing the entrance on the southeast corner, toward the neighborhood; and by creating a visual water/fire asset at that juncture to be enjoyed by the adjoining townhouses. St. James Street was further protected because the automated parking system required no ramps and therefore no traffic on St. James Street.

Window wall systems on the building's north and northeast facades act as a neutral backdrop to the historical context to the north side. The south and southeast facades are a combination of metal panel and glass configured to respond to Society Hill's residential patterns.

500 Walnut established a new economic platform for residential development in Philadelphia, and its economic success has become a local legend.

Norman and Suzanne Cohn
Norman and Suzanne Cohn have had an enormous impact on my career as an architect. Our meeting in 2004 was serendipitous. Allan Domb, a Philadelphia real estate developer, had purchased the vacant 21-story Jewish Federation Building at 1601 Locust Street and retained Cecil Baker & Associates to remake it as a luxury condominium building, subsequently christened the Lanesborough. The building's floor plate allowed for one 3,500-square-foot apartment per floor, each served by a private elevator lobby and offering views in three directions. As part of the architectural commission, Allan asked us to design one of the sample units.

About this time, the Cohns were looking for an urban pied-à-terre. After visiting the Lanesborough's model unit, they hired us to evaluate other possibilities based on their intuition that they had found a kindred design spirit. We subsequently designed, and saw through construction, three homes for the Cohns – a penthouse on the 45th floor of the St. James in Society Hill; a penthouse in Naples, Florida; and the reconfiguration and rehabilitation of a summer house in Harvey Cedars, New Jersey.

All these residences blur the distinction between home, museum, and sanctuary. The Cohns inspire the designers, builders, and artisans to submit their very best work. This is as close as I have come to perfection.

"Baker's firm is known for designing private residences with significant art collections, and the Cohns' Naples condo was no exception. Equally important to the spectacular view was how the couple's extensive collection, particularly their glass art, would be showcased. Longtime patrons of the visual arts, the Cohns wanted their home to function as a gallery. And with limited wall space thanks to those massive windows, it was essential they plan art placement from the start. 'We are always looking for a unified fluency between home and gallery, so one doesn't overpower the other,' says Baker, who wants his clients to be comfortable but also highly attuned to the art within. 'Suzanne Cohn is a master of that dance,' he says. 'She understands the importance of keeping the domestic elements in harmony with the art.'"

"Baker got to know the Cohns' collection before drawing up plans. He and Suzanne would discuss where pieces might go in the home, but Suzanne would also surprise Baker with new acquisitions like the large ghost-like light Gweilo by Parachilna in the living room, which Baker immediately redesigned the room to accommodate. 'Certain spaces went through a lot of iterations,' Suzanne says. 'He designed the bones for the interior – exactly the right shape and space for the art.'" Gulfshore Life, Home Spring, 2002.

Suzanne Cohn has me crossing thresholds that are unbeknownst to me, challenging me to think in ways outside my comfort zone. When finished, I do not know the provenance of the solution: Was it Suzanne? Was it me? And Norman, with quiet grace, seconds and supports the vision.

I have been very lucky.

COLLABORATORS & PROJECT CREDITS

When my mind wanders to the people who have been so much a part of my vocational world my stomach muscles tighten. I am aware that I was often an unfocused partner and a distant boss. In that part of the world I inhabited I was selfishly fenced in by my craft. I was playing in my own sandlot, intruders largely unwelcome. Yet I was surrounded by amazing collaborators, who, in the end, made me a much better businessman and architect.

Amongst them (I know I am sadly missing many additional names):

Elliot Rothschild, Mike Horn, Alden Blyth.
Our partners at BRHB: Olin Belsinger, Ted Robb, Ed Deering.

Nancy Bastian, Eric Leighton, Chris Blakelock.

Jim Wolters, Bill Cheeseman, Kate Cleveland, Jim Cornwall, Janice Woodcock, Alexandra Fazio, Ray Klumb, Shep Houston, Maureen Carlson, Muhammad Ali, Joe Denegre, Kevin Blackney, Alice Chung, John Hayes, Michael Hauptmann, Dave Brawer, Lloyd Chu, John Howard, Roland Smith, Bodhi Knott, Penny Marvel, Stephen Verner, James Ruckman, Jeff Lineman, Brian Johnston, Sui San Mui, Rebecca Frisch, Kathryn Kelly, Jacob Gulesian, Daniel Brown, Jenna Shuster, Nah Jeong Yeh, Ann LaBorie, Gordon Fluke, Rohit Arora, Mohammad Saleem, Kirsten Carangi, Nick Marchek, Kevin Towey, Aaron Miller, Jack Larimore, Ryan Hill, Carl Emberger, Michael Fierle, David Daniels, Paonsiri Yuvaves, Lauren Karwoski Magee, Kacy Wander, Nicholas Connolly, Nora Bergsten, Dan Kayser, Carolina Gallegos Navarro, Robyn Savacool, Zephyr Martin, Kara Kray, Sharvari Mhatre, Banu Altman.

And those that helped manage us:
Nana Lee, Marge Shernecke, Olivier Dunrae, Joan Wetmore, Rachel Plaisted, Marge Carango, Kristin Langford, Mary Tasillo, Dennis Pilsits

And the gentle soul that took care of us:
Stanley Watson

The Nest
Owner: Bock Development Group
Architect: Cecil Baker + Partners
Project Team: Cecil Baker, Chris Blakelock,
Aaron Miller, Ryan Hill, Jack Larimore
Structural Engineer: Michael Baker Associates
Lighting Designer: BEAM
GC: Ernest Bock & Sons
Completed: 2018
Photographer: Barry Halkin

Sag Harbor Residence
Project brought to Cecil Baker & Associates by
Alexandra Fazio
Architect: Cecil Baker & Associates
Project Team: Cecil Baker, Alexandra Fazio,
Chris Blakelock
GC: Greg D'Angelo Construction
Completed: 2010
Photographer: Michael Grim; Thomas Loof;
Cecil Baker; Alexandra Fazio

York Square
Owner: Berkshire Construction Management -
Mark Hallowell and Paul Horning
Architect: Cecil Baker & Associates
Project Team: Cecil Baker, Kevin Towey,
Jeff Linneman
Landscape Architect: Margie Ruddick
Landscape Architect
Structural Engineer: O'Donnell & Naccarato
GC: Skanska USA, Construction Manager
Completed: 2006
Photographer: Barry Halkin; Cecil Baker

The Lippincott
Owner: MCW Properties, Jay Cranmer and
Mike Merkle
Architect: Cecil Baker & Associates
Project Team: Cecil Baker, Steve Verner, Chris
Blakelock, Penny Marvel
Structural Engineer: The Harman Group
Lighting Designer; BEAM; Tigue Lighting
GC: J. J. deLuca Company, Inc.
Completed: 2010
Photographer: Barry Halkin; Joe Kitchen; Cecil Baker

Van Pelt Mews
Owner: The Conservatory Group with Andrew Kamins
Architect: Cecil Baker + Partners
Project Team: Cecil Baker, Eric Leighton, Ryan Hill
Structural Engineer: Conn Shaffer Consulting Engineers
Completed: 2016
Photographer: Barry Halkin; Cecil Baker;
Oscar Riera Ojeda

Urban Townhouses
Architect: Cecil Baker & Associates
Project Team: Cecil Baker
Landscape Architect: Piedmont Design; Anna Prinzo
Structural Engineer: O'Donnell & Naccarato
GC: Hoekenga/Baker
Completed: 2000
Photographer: Barry Halkin; Tom Crane; David Eichler;
Cecil Baker

Jannie's Place
Owner: HopePHL
(formerly People's Emergency Center)
Housing Consultant: Stone Sherick Consulting
Architect: Cecil Baker & Associates
Project Team: Cecil Baker, Chris Blakelock
Structural Engineer: The Harman Group
GC: Allied Construction
Completed: 2011
Photographer: Joe Kitchen; Cecil Baker

Fire Engine #37
Owners: Department of Public Property, Philadelphia, PA
Architect: Cecil Baker + Partners
Project Team: Cecil Baker, Eric Leighton, Nicholas
Connolly, Carolina Gallegos Navarro
Lighting Designer: BEAM
Structural Engineer: Ann Rothmann
1% Art: Firefighter's Arc by Erica Ehrenbard and
Jill Sablosky
GC: Magnum
Completed: 2022
Photographer: Barry Halkin; Cecil Baker

Suzanne & Norman Cohn Philadelphia City Residence
Architect: Cecil Baker & Associates
Project Team: Cecil Baker, Stephen Verner, Nicholas
Marchek, Penny Marvel
Lighting Designer: BEAM
GC: Wolfe Scott
Completed: 2008
Photographer: Barry Halkin

500 Walnut
Owner: Scannapieco Development Corporation.
Tom Scannapieco, Rod Werner, Paula Barron
Architect: Cecil Baker & Associates,
Cecil Baker + Partners
Project team: Cecil Baker, Eric Leighton, Ryan Hill, Dan Kayser, Jack Larimore, Alexandra Fazio
Interior Design: Janet Espenshade and
Cecil Baker + Partners
Structural Engineer: WSP Group
Lighting Designer: BEAM
Landscape Architect: Mahan Rykal Associates
GC: Intech
Completed: 2017
Photographer: Barry Halkin; David Fonda;
Cecil Baker

Horseshoe Bay Residence
Architect: Cecil Baker + Partners
Project Team: Cecil Baker, Eric Leighton
Structural Engineer: Structures Inc
Landscape Architect: Will Pickens
GC: Dauphine Homes
Completed: 2012
Photographer: Paul Bardagjy; Sam Drago;
Cecil Baker

Kol Emet
Owner: Building Committee: Tom Kearns, Barbara and Steve Gross, Ellie Fisher, et al.
Architect: Cecil Baker & Associates
Project Team: Cecil Baker, Janice Woodcock, Bodhi Knott
Structural Engineers: Ann Rothmann
Lighting Designer: BEAM
GC: Branch Valley
Completed 2000
Photographer: Barry Halkin; Cecil Baker

Mission Green
Owner: Medical Mission Sisters and Inglis Housing Corporation. Sister Frankie Vaughan, PM.
Housing Consultant: Diamond and Associates
Architect: Cecil Baker + Partners
Project Team: Cecil Baker, Nick Marchek
Lighting Designer: BEAM
Structural Engineer: The Harman Group
Completed: 2014
Photography: Joe Kitchen

Western Union Condominiums
Owner: Campenella Development/Moreland Development/Thylan Associates
Architect: Cecil Baker & Associates
Project Team: Cecil Baker, Eric Leighton, Paonsiri Yuvaves, Penny Marvel
Structural Engineers: O'Donnell & Naccarato
GC: Campenella Construction
Completed: 2009
Photographer: Barry Halkin; Cecil Baker

Hilarie and Mitchell Morgan Residence
Architect: Cecil Baker + Partners
Project Team: Cecil Baker, David Daniels, Carolina Gallegos Navarro, Jack Larimore
Interior Designer: Ken Alpert
GC: Shay Construction, Inc.
Completed: 2018
Photographer: Barry Halkin; Gianni Franchellucci

St. Rita Place and Cascia Center
Owner: Catholic Housing & Community Services
Housing Consultant: Diamond & Associates
Architect: Cecil Baker + Partners
Project Team: Cecil Baker, Nancy Bastian, Nora Bergsten
Structural Engineer: Keast & Hood
Lighting Designer: BEAM
GC: Domus
Completed: 2021
Photographer: Barry Halkin; Cecil Baker

Durovsik Residence
Architect: Cecil Baker + Partners
(project transferred by Owners from another architect. Cecil Baker + Partners kept the general layout but redesigned the residence)
Project Team: Cecil Baker, Nicholas Connolly, Carolina Gallegos Navarro, Jack Larimore
Interior Designer: Pia Halloran / BGD Design
Structural Engineer: Tim Beaver
Lighting Designer: Filament 33, Marianne Maloney
GC: Shay Construction, Inc.
Completed: 2023
Photographer: Barry Halkin; Cecil Baker

Andrew R. And Mindy H. Heyer Lobby
Owner: University of Pennsylvania School of Veterinary Medicine
Architect: Cecil Baker + Partners
Project Team: Cecil Baker, Nancy Bastian, Nora Bergsten, Chris Blakelock
Lighting Designer: BEAM
GC: Canuso Jordan
Completed: 2015
Photographer: Barry Halkin

Chestnut Hill Library Addition
Owner: Free Library of Philadelphia
Architect: Cecil Baker & Associates
Project team: Cecil Baker, Nancy Bastian, Joe Denegre
Landscape Architect: Ed Boyer
Structural Engineer: O'Donnell & Naccarato
GC: Intech
Completed: 1996
Photographer: Tom Crane

Suzanne & Norman Cohn, Primary Residence
Architect: Cecil Baker + Partners
Project Team: Cecil Baker, Aaron Miller, Jack Larimore
Lighting Designer: BEAM
GC: BUILD
Completed: 2021
Photographer: Barry Halkin; Tina Sargent

Riverview Executive Park
Owner: LaMelza Enterprises
Architect: Cecil Baker & Associates
Project Team: Cecil Baker, Kevin Blackney, Jim Wolters, John Howard
Land Planner and Landscape Architect: Wells Appel
Structural Engineer: O'Donnell & Naccarato
GC: R. M. Shoemaker
Completed: 1990
Photographer: The Leigh Photographic Group; Matt Wargo; Tom Bernard

Society Hill Residence
Architect: Cecil Baker + Partners
Project Team: Cecil Baker, Ryan Hill
GC: Hallowell Construction
Completed: 2023
Photographer: Barry Halkin; Cecil Baker

Jefferson Accelerator Zone
Owner: Thomas Jefferson University
Architect: Cecil Baker + Partners
Project Team: Cecil Baker, Chris Blakelock
Lighting designer: BEAM
Completed: 2014
Photographer: Matt Wargo

One Riverside
Owner: Dranoff Properties. Carl Dranoff, Michael Asnes, Marianne Harris
Architect: Cecil Baker + Partners
Project Team: Cecil Baker, Nancy Bastian, Carl Emberger, Michael Fierle, Jack Larimore
Landscape Architect: Studio Bryan Hanes
Lighting Designer: BEAM
Structural Engineer: The Harman Group
GC: Intech
Completed: 2017
Photographer: Barry Halkin; David Fonda; Don Pearse; Oscar Riera Ojeda; Cecil Baker

Bridgette Mayer Gallery
Architect: Cecil Baker + Partners
Project team: Cecil Baker, Eric Leighton, Nick Marchek
Lighting designer: Andrew Slavinskas
GC: Hanson, Kevin McDonnell
Completed: 2011
Photographer: Barry Halkin

2100 Hamilton
Owner: Bock Development Group. Tom Bock, Denise Collins
Architect: Cecil Baker + Partners
Project Team: Cecil Baker, Chris Blakelock, Ryan Hill, Aaron Miller, Jack Larimore
Landscape Architect: Sikora Wells Appel
Structural Engineer: Thornton Tomasetti
CC: Ernest Bock & Sons
Completed: 2023
Photographer: Barry Halkin; David Fonda; Cecil Baker

Buck and Weinberg Residence Halls, Northern Home for Children
Owner: Northern Children
Architect: Cecil Baker & Associates
Project Team: Cecil Baker, Nancy Bastian, Penny Marvel, Lauren Karwoski Magee, Ryan Drummond
Landscape Architect: Ralph Sauer & Partners (Buck); Veridian (Weinberg)
Structural Engineer: Bevan Lawson
GC: Flatiron (Buck); Domus (Weinberg)
Completed: Buck Residence, 2001; Weinberg Residence, 2009
Photographer: Barry Halkin

Fretz Showroom
Owner: Fretz Corp.
Architect: Cecil Baker + Partners
Project Team: Cecil Baker, Eric Leighton, Ryan Hill, Alexandra Fazio
Interior Designer: Michael Murtha
Structural Engineer: Conn Shaffer
Lighting Designer: BEAM
GC: Wolfe Scott
Completed: 2012
Photographer: Barry Halkin

Police Fire Headquarters
Owner: Capital Projects Office of the City of Philadelphia. David Viella, Fredda Lippes, Gary Knappick
Architect: Cecil Baker & Associates
Project Team: Cecil Baker, Jim Wolters, Bill Cheeseman, Janice Woodcock, Roland Smith
Landscape Architect: Lager Raabe
1% Art: Stacy Levy
Structural Engineer: O'Donnell and Naccarato
Completed: 2000
Photographer: Barry Halkin

JCHAI
Owner: Judith Creed Horizons for Achieving Independence (JCHAI)
Architect: Cecil Baker + Partners
Project team: Cecil Baker, Eric Leighton, Aaron Miller
Lighting Designer: BEAM
Structural Engineer: Ann Rothmann
GC: Terra Firma Builders
Completed: 2021
Photographer: Jack Zignon; Cecil Baker; Aaron Miller

Fire Engine #38
Owner: City of Philadelphia Department of Public Property
Architect: Cecil Baker + Partners
Project team: Cecil Baker, Eric Leighton, Chris Blakelock, Kacy Wander
Landscape Architect: Veridian Landscape Studio
Structural Engineer: Ann Rothmann
GC: Little Builders
Completed: 2016
Photographer: Barry Halkin

Ralston/Mercy-Douglass House
Owner: RalstonHouse & Mercy-Douglass; School of Nursing, University Pennsylvania
Housing Consultant: Ted Robb and Burt Weiner
Architect: Cecil Baker & Associates
Project team: Cecil Baker, Nancy Bastian
Landscape Architect: Margaret S. Judd
Structural Engineer: O'Donnell & Naccarato
GC: Daniel Keating
Completed: 2001
Photographer: Barry Halkin; Cecil Baker

Rolling Stock Hall
Architect: Cecil Baker & Associates
Project Team: Cecil Baker, Jim Wolters, John Howard, Nancy Bastian
Structural Engineer: O'Donnell & Naccarato
Completed: 1995
Photographer: Lori Stahl

2110 Walnut Street
Owner: Astoban Investments LLC
Architect: Cecil Baker + Partners
Project Team: Cecil Baker, Eric Leighton, Nicholas Connolly, Carolina Gallegos Navarro
Structural Engineer: Larsen & Landis
GC: Dale Corporation & Urban Space Development
Completed: 2018
Photographer: Barry Halkin; Better World Photography: Cecil Baker

New Courtland Allegheny Campus
Owner: NewCourtland Senior Services.
Client contact: Max Kent
Housing Consultant: Stone Sherick Consulting
Architect: Cecil Baker + Partners
Project Team: Cecil Baker, Nancy Bastian, Chris Blakelock, Ryan Hill
Lighting Designer: BEAM
Structural Engineer: The Harman Group

Great Hills Corporate Center
Owner: Landmark Associates
Architect: Cecil Baker & Associates
Project team: Cecil Baker, Ray Klumb, Kevin Blackney
Land Planner, Landscape Architect: John Rahenkamp & Associates
Structural Engineer: O'Donnell Naccarato
GC: Arbor Corporation
Completed: 1988
Photographer: Greg Hursley

Candy Factory Court
Owner: Fairley and Cecil Baker
Project Team: Cecil Baker
GC: BRHB Developers
Completed: 1978
Photographer: Tom Crane,

Inglis Methodist Gardens
Owner: Inglis Housing Corporation and Methodist Services
Project Architect: Cecil Baker + Partners
Project Team: Cecil Baker, Ryan Hill, Robyn Savacool
GC: Domus
Completion: 2021
Photographer: Barry Halkin

The Waterworks
Owner: River Road Development; Tom Scannapieco, President
Architect: Cecil Baker & Associates
Project Team: Cecil Baker, Bill Cheeseman, Joe Denegre, James Ruckman
Landscape Architect: Ed Boyer
Structural Engineer: O'Donnell & Naccarato
Completed: 1988
Photographer: James d'Addio

Turning on the Lights Upstairs
Client: CCD. Paul Levy, Executive Director, CCD; Nancy Goldenberg, Project Manager
Funding provided by The Pew Charitable Trusts
Architect: Cecil Baker & Associates
Project Team: Cecil Baker, Janice Woodcock
Development Consultant: Eugene LeFevre
Completed: 1996

Cover photograph: Oscar Riera Ojeda

BOOK CREDITS

Graphic Design
Juan Pablo Sarrabayrouse

Art Direction
Oscar Riera Ojeda

Copy Editing
Kit Maude

OSCAR RIERA OJEDA
PUBLISHERS

Copyright 2025 Oscar Riera Ojeda Publishers Limited
ISBN 978-1-964490-08-3
Published by Oscar Riera Ojeda Publishers Limited
Printed in China

Oscar Riera Ojeda Publishers Limited
Unit 1331, Beverley Commercial Centre,
87-105 Chatham Road South, Tsim Sha Tsui, Kowloon, Hong Kong

Production Offices
Suit 19, Shenyun Road,
Nanshan District, Shenzhen 518055, China

International Customer Service & Editorial Questions: +1-484-502-5400

www.oropublishers.com | www.oscarrieraojeda.com
oscar@oscarrieraojeda.com

All rights reserved. No part of this book may be reproduced, stored in a retrieval system, or transmitted in any form or by any means, including electronic, mechanical, photocopying of microfilming, recording, or otherwise (except that copying permitted by Sections 107 and 108 of the U.S. Copyright Law and except by reviewers for the public press) without written permission from the publisher.